ARCTIC MONKEYS

Music transcriptions by Addi Booth, Aurelien Budynek, Jeff Jacobson and David Stocker

ISBN 978-1-4803-6400-4

7777 W. BLUEMOUND RD. P.O. BOX 13819 MILWAUKEE, WI 53213

In Australia Contact:
Hal Leonard Australia Pty. Ltd.
4 Lentara Court
Cheltenham, Victoria, 3192 Australia
Email: ausadmin@halleonard.com.au

For all works contained herein:
Unauthorized copying, arranging, adapting, recording, Internet posting, public performance,
or other distribution of the printed music in this publication is an infringement of copyright.
Infringers are liable under the law.

Visit Hal Leonard Online at
www.halleonard.com

ARCTIC MONKEYS

Page	Title
5	DO I WANNA KNOW?
15	R U MINE?
24	ONE FOR THE ROAD
33	ARABELLA
41	I WANT IT ALL
46	NO. 1 PARTY ANTHEM
58	MAD SOUNDS
64	FIRESIDE
70	WHY'D YOU ONLY CALL ME WHEN YOU'RE HIGH?
79	SNAP OUT OF IT
87	KNEE SOCKS
96	I WANNA BE YOURS
103	Guitar Notation Legend

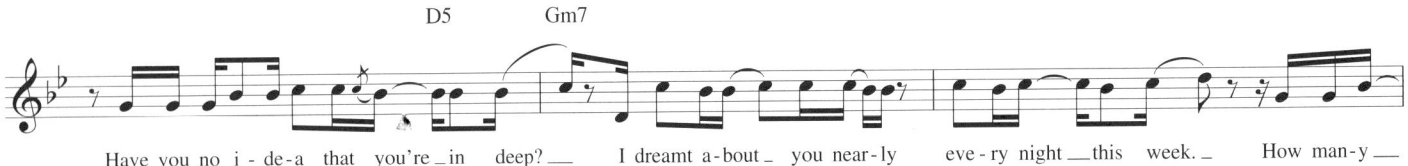

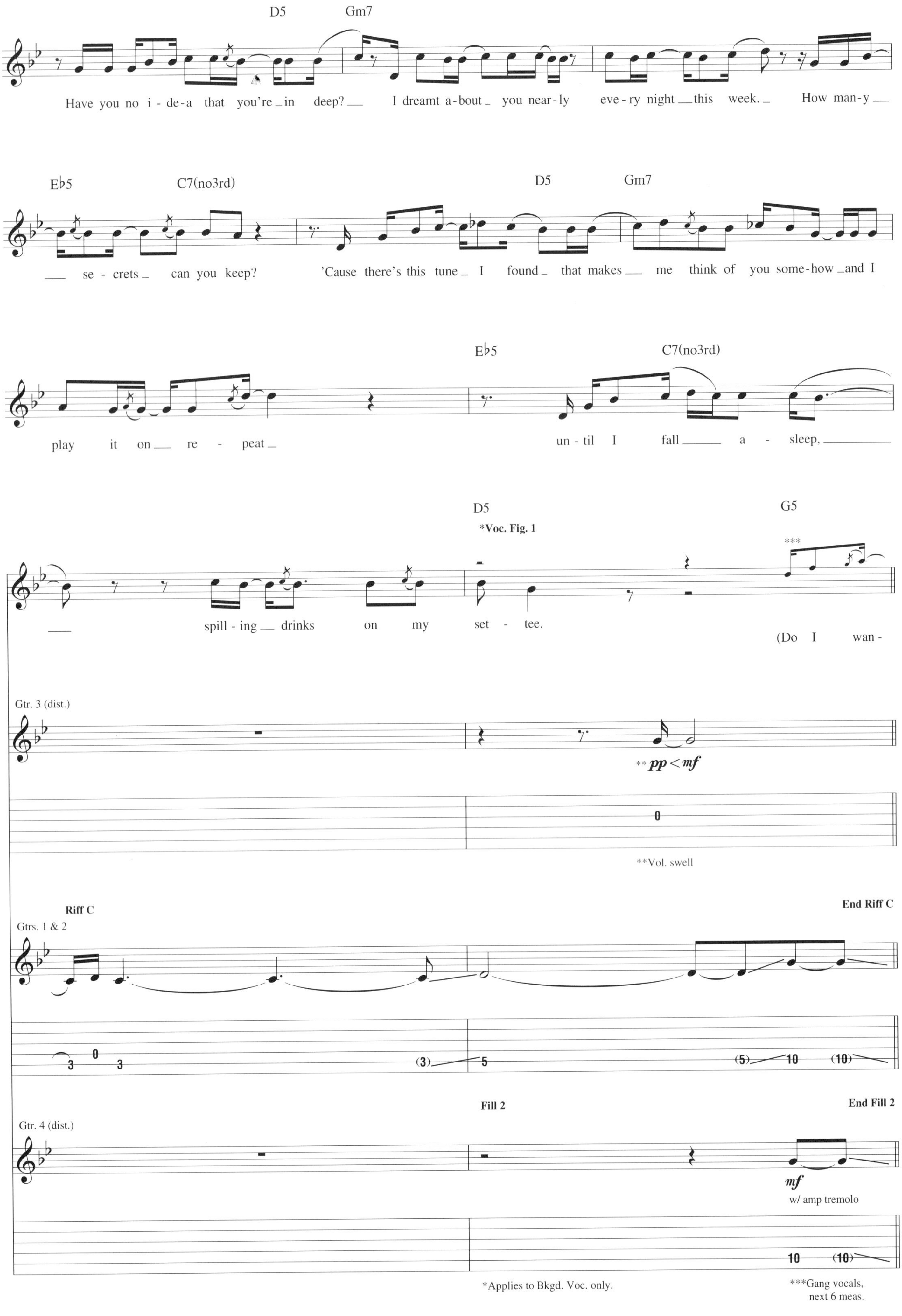
D5 Gm7
Have you no i-de-a that you're in deep? I dreamt a-bout you near-ly eve-ry night this week. How man-y
Eb5 C7(no3rd) D5 Gm7
se-crets can you keep? 'Cause there's this tune I found that makes me think of you some-how and I
Eb5 C7(no3rd)
play it on re-peat un-til I fall a-sleep,
D5 G5
*Voc. Fig. 1
spill-ing drinks on my set-tee.
(Do I wan-
Gtr. 3 (dist.)
**pp < mf
**Vol. swell
Riff C
End Riff C
Gtrs. 1 & 2
Fill 2
End Fill 2
Gtr. 4 (dist.)
mf
w/ amp tremolo
*Applies to Bkgd. Voc. only.
***Gang vocals, next 6 meas.

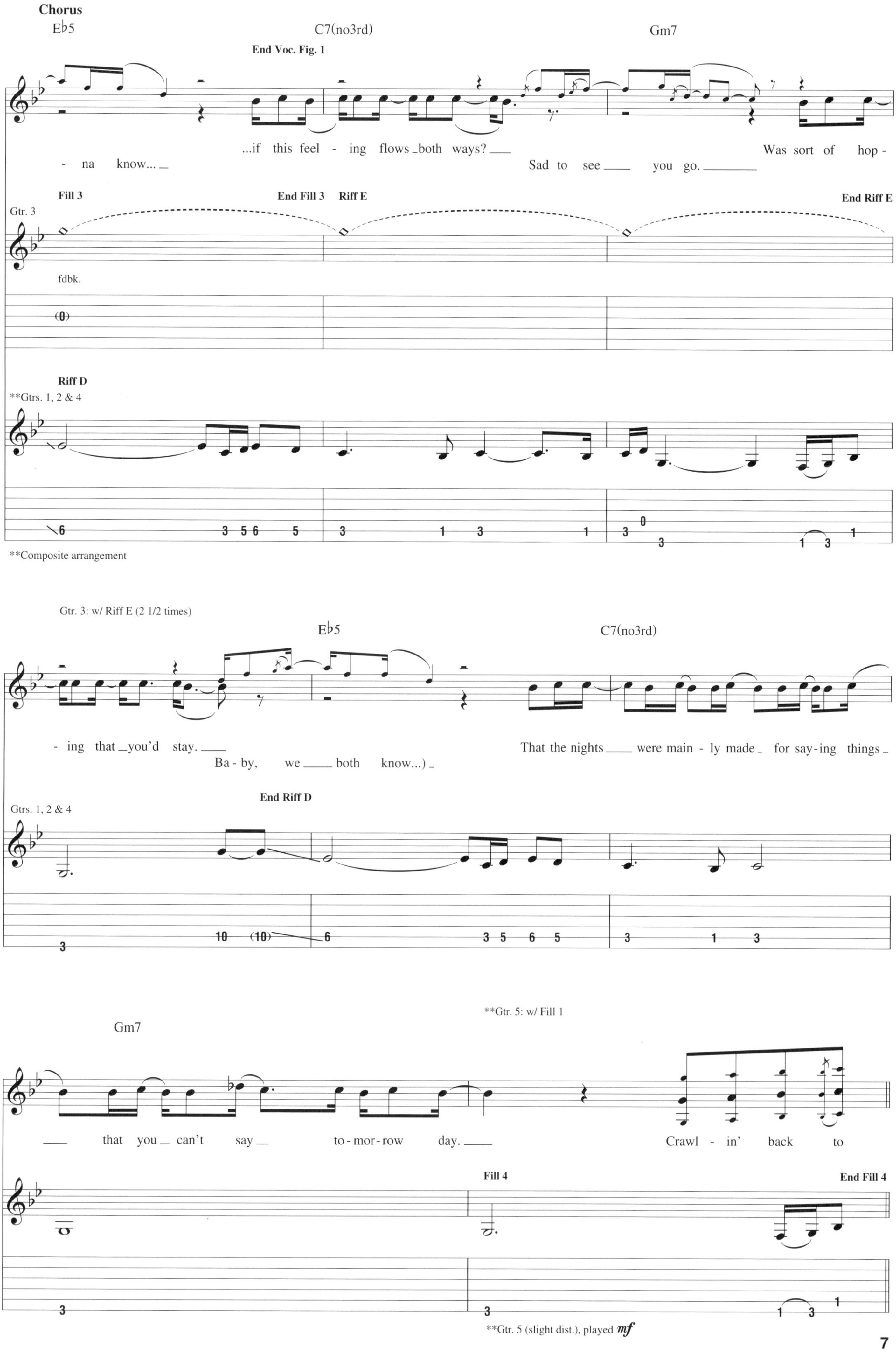
Chorus
E♭5
C7(no3rd)
Gm7
End Voc. Fig. 1
...if this feel - ing flows both ways?
Sad to see you go.
Was sort of hop -
- na know...
Fill 3
End Fill 3
Riff E
End Riff E
Gtr. 3
fdbk.
Riff D
**Gtrs. 1, 2 & 4
**Composite arrangement
Gtr. 3: w/ Riff E (2 1/2 times)
E♭5
C7(no3rd)
- ing that you'd stay.
Ba - by, we both know...)
That the nights were main - ly made for say-ing things
End Riff D
Gtrs. 1, 2 & 4
Gm7
**Gtr. 5: w/ Fill 1
that you can't say to-mor-row day.
Crawl - in' back to
Fill 4
End Fill 4
**Gtr. 5 (slight dist.), played mf

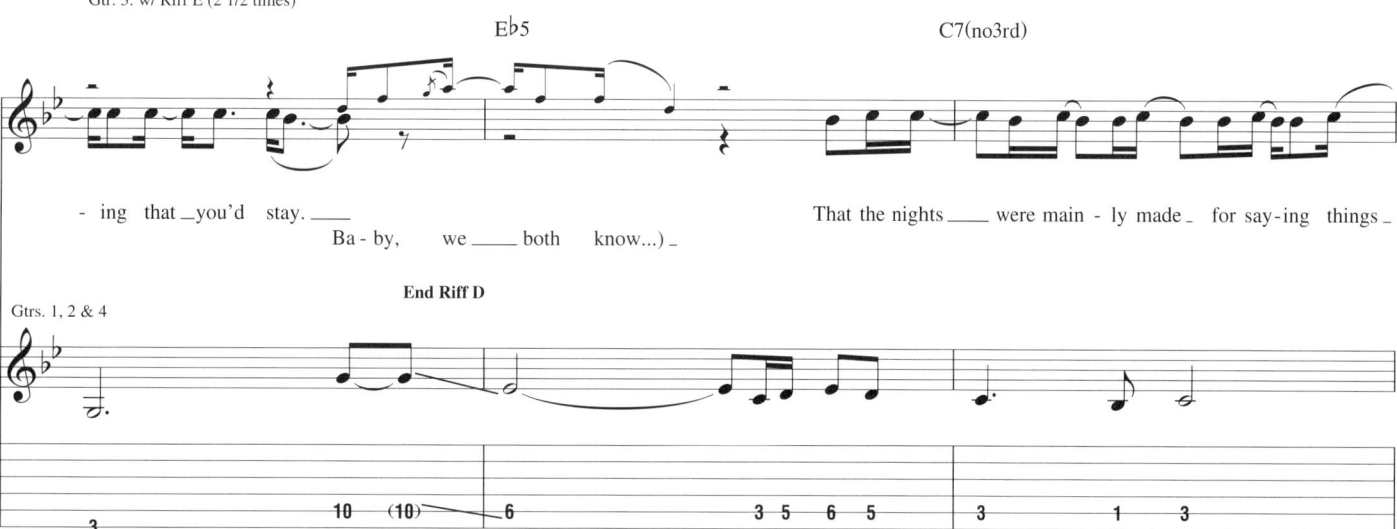

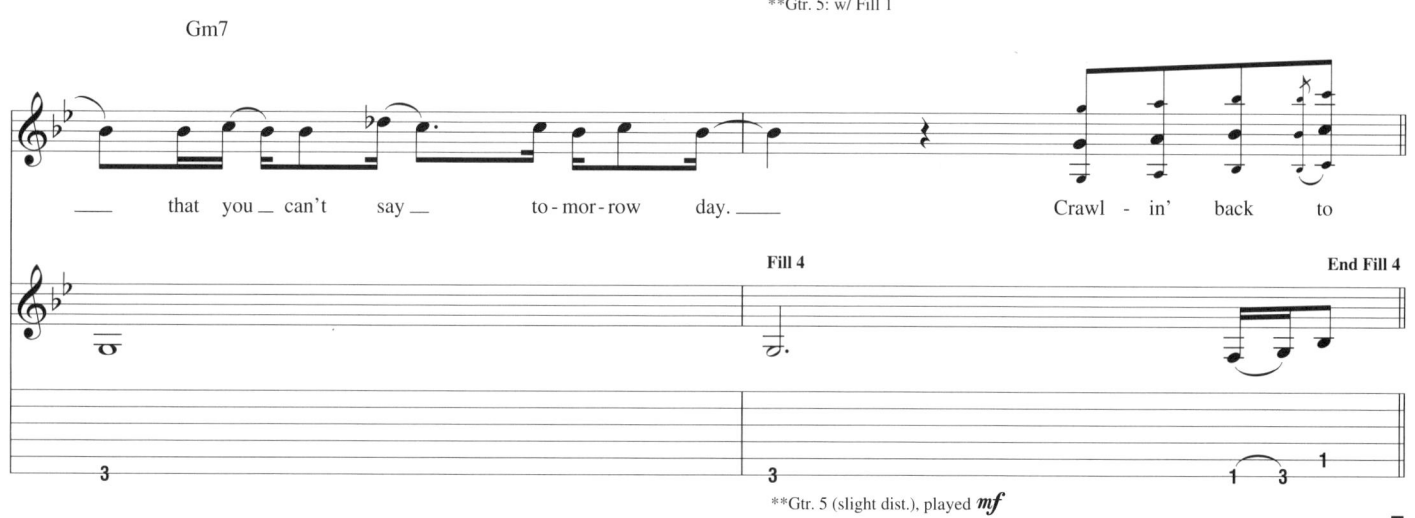

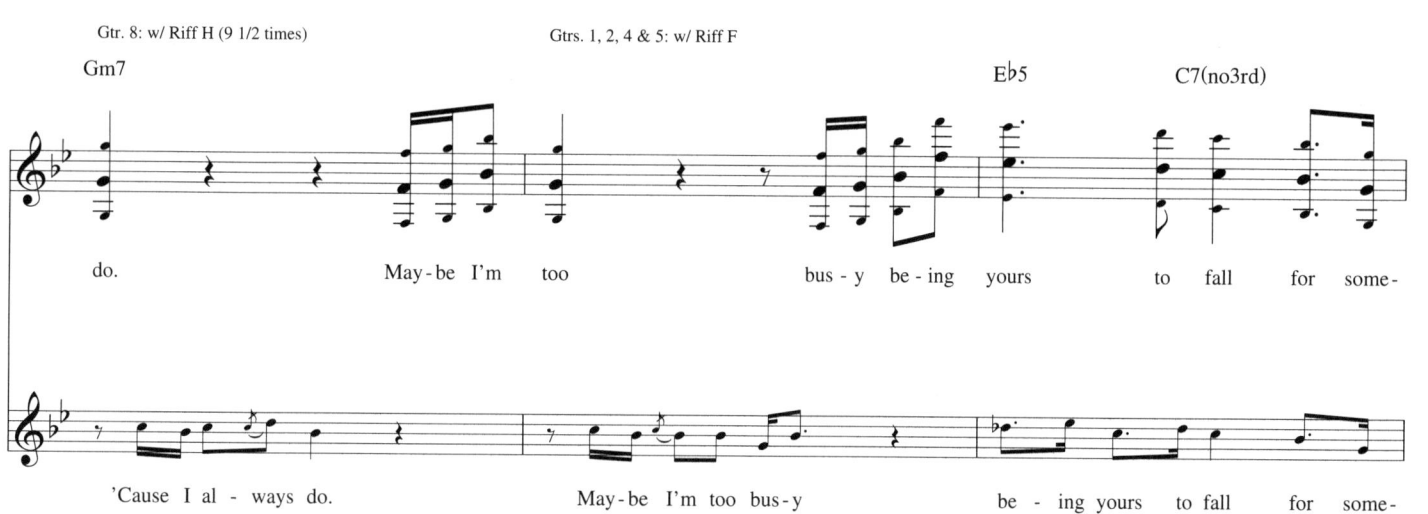

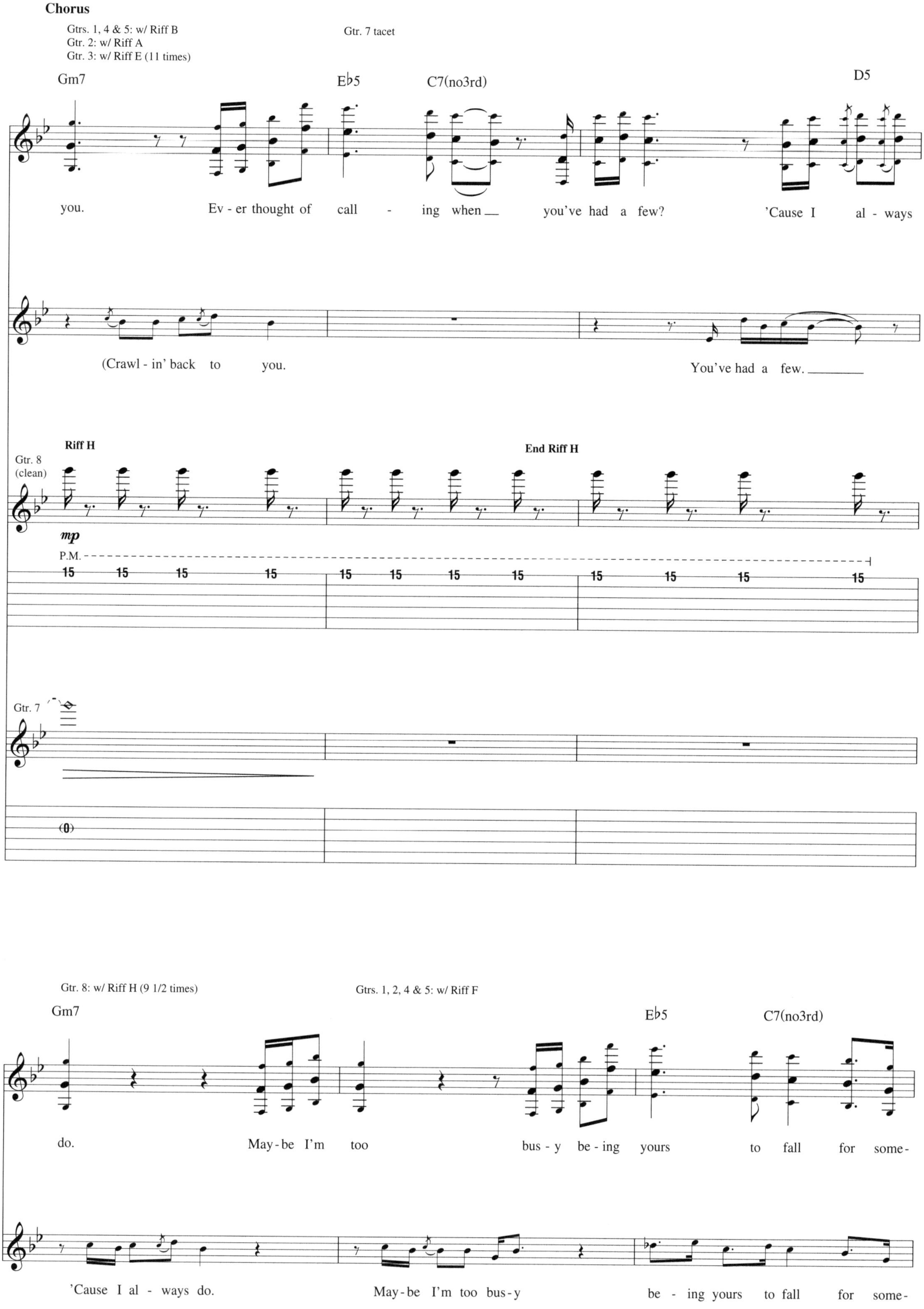
Chorus
Gtrs. 1, 4 & 5: w/ Riff B
Gtr. 2: w/ Riff A
Gtr. 3: w/ Riff E (11 times)
Gtr. 7 tacet
Gm7
E♭5
C7(no3rd)
D5
you. Ev - er thought of call - ing when you've had a few? 'Cause I al - ways
(Crawl - in' back to you.
You've had a few.
Riff H
End Riff H
Gtr. 8 (clean)
mp
P.M.
15 15 15 15 15 15 15 15 15 15 15 15
Gtr. 7
(0)
Gtr. 8: w/ Riff H (9 1/2 times)
Gtrs. 1, 2, 4 & 5: w/ Riff F
Gm7
E♭5
C7(no3rd)
do. May - be I'm too bus - y be - ing yours to fall for some -
'Cause I al - ways do.
May - be I'm too bus - y
be - ing yours to fall for some -

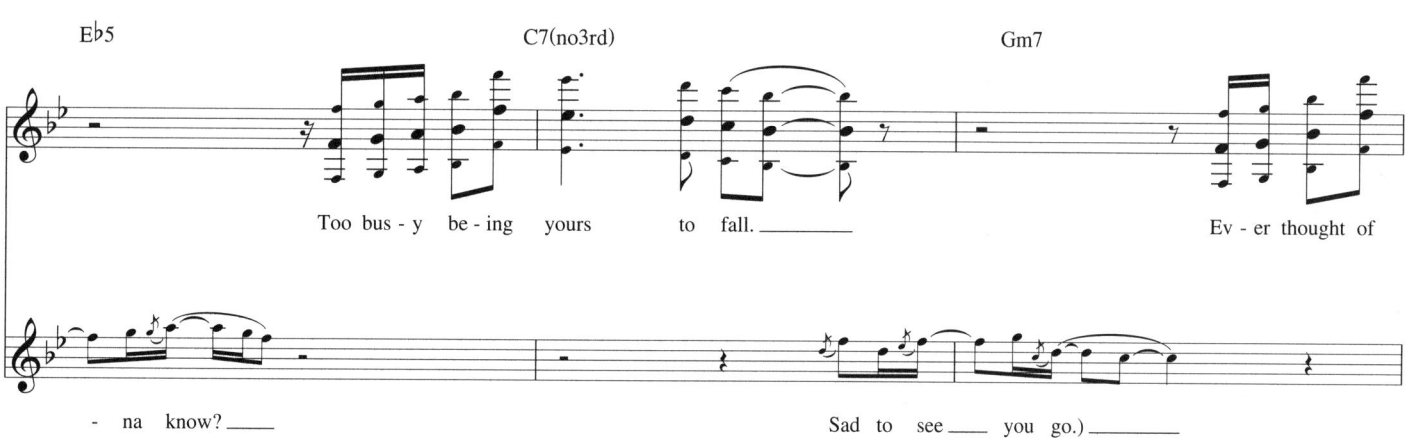
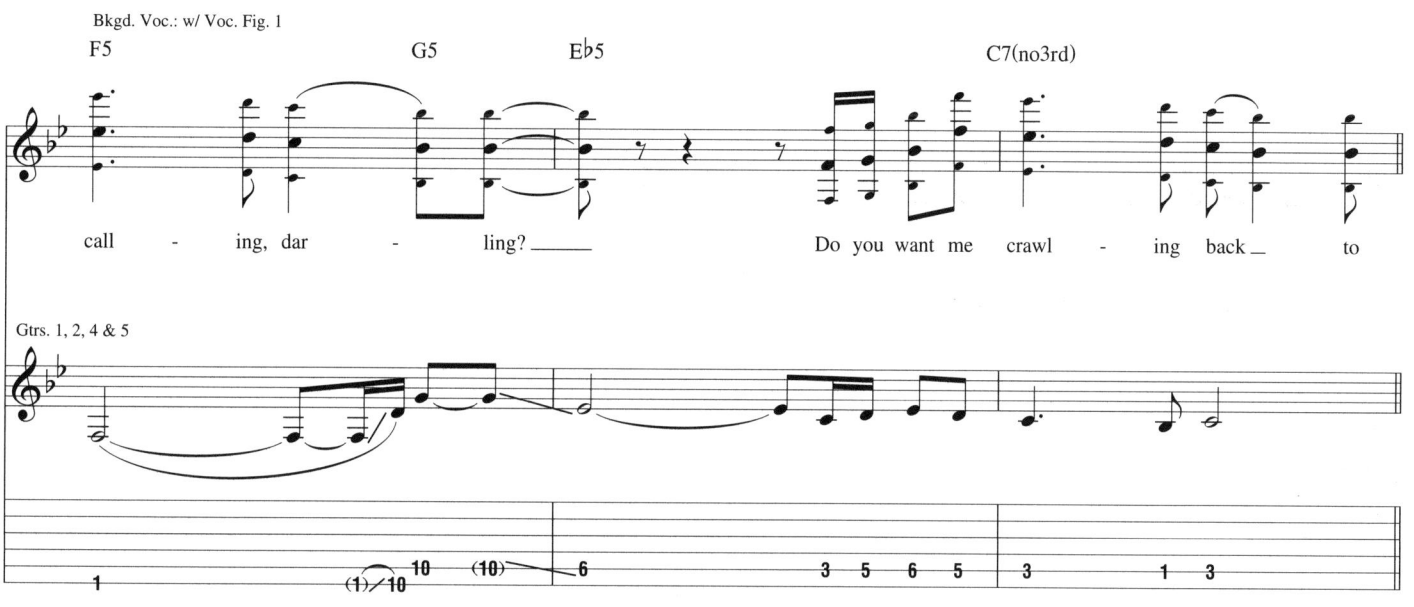

R U Mine?

Words by Alex Turner
Music by Arctic Monkeys

*Chord symbols reflect implied harmony.

© 2013 EMI MUSIC PUBLISHING LTD.
All Rights in the U.S. and Canada Controlled and Administered by EMI APRIL MUSIC INC. and EMI BLACKWOOD MUSIC INC.
All Rights Reserved   International Copyright Secured   Used by Permission

15

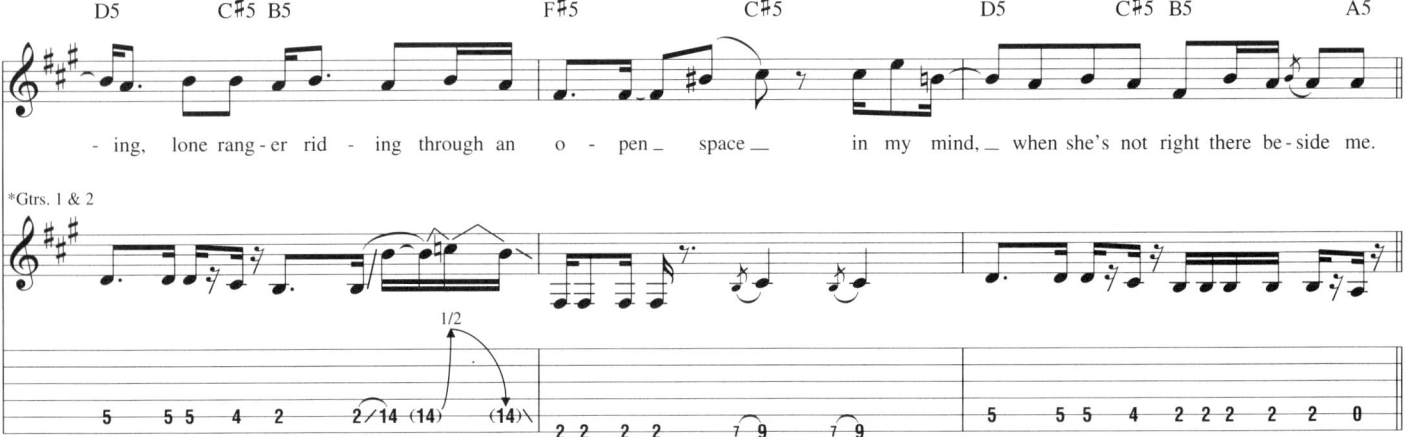

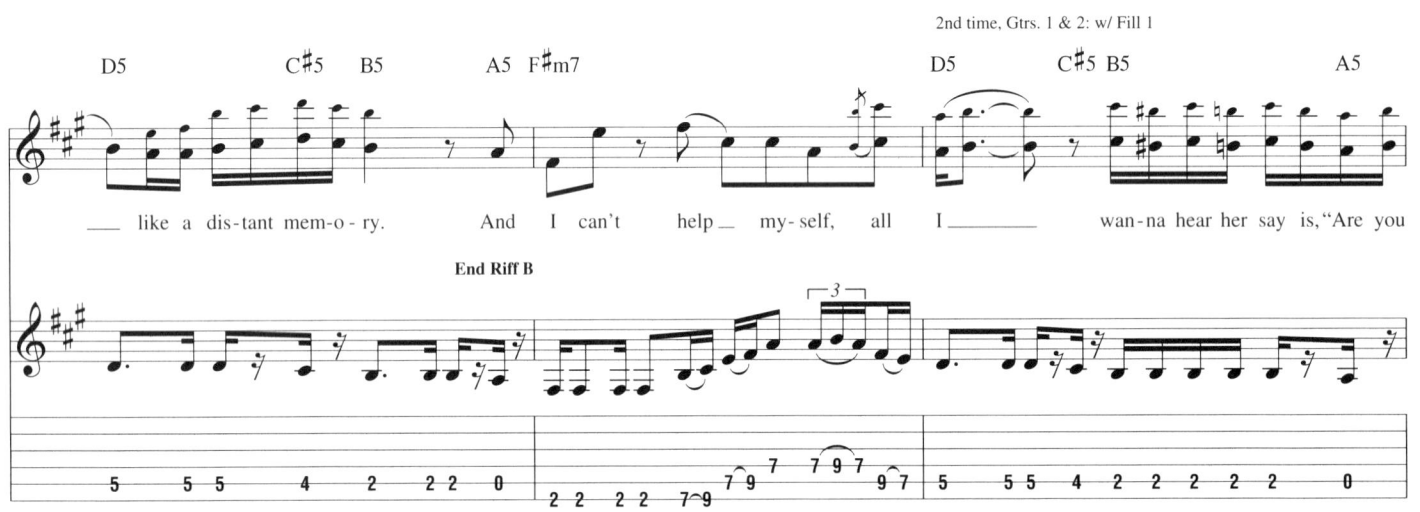

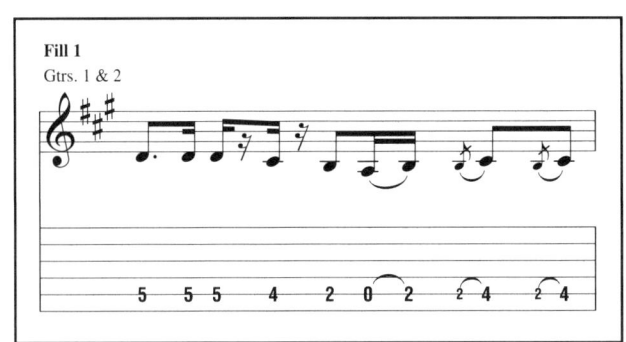

To Coda
Gtrs. 1 & 2: w/ Riff B
F♯m7
D5
C♯5
B5
A5
mine?"
*Sung behind the beat.
Well, are you
Chorus
F♯5
N.C.
D5
C♯5
B5
A5
F♯5
N.C.
mine?
Are you
mine?
Riff C
End Riff C
Gtrs. 1 & 2
D5
C♯5
B5
A5
F♯5
D5
C♯5
B5
A5
Are you
mine?
Are
you.
Gtr. 1
w/ bar
Gtr. 2
w/ bar

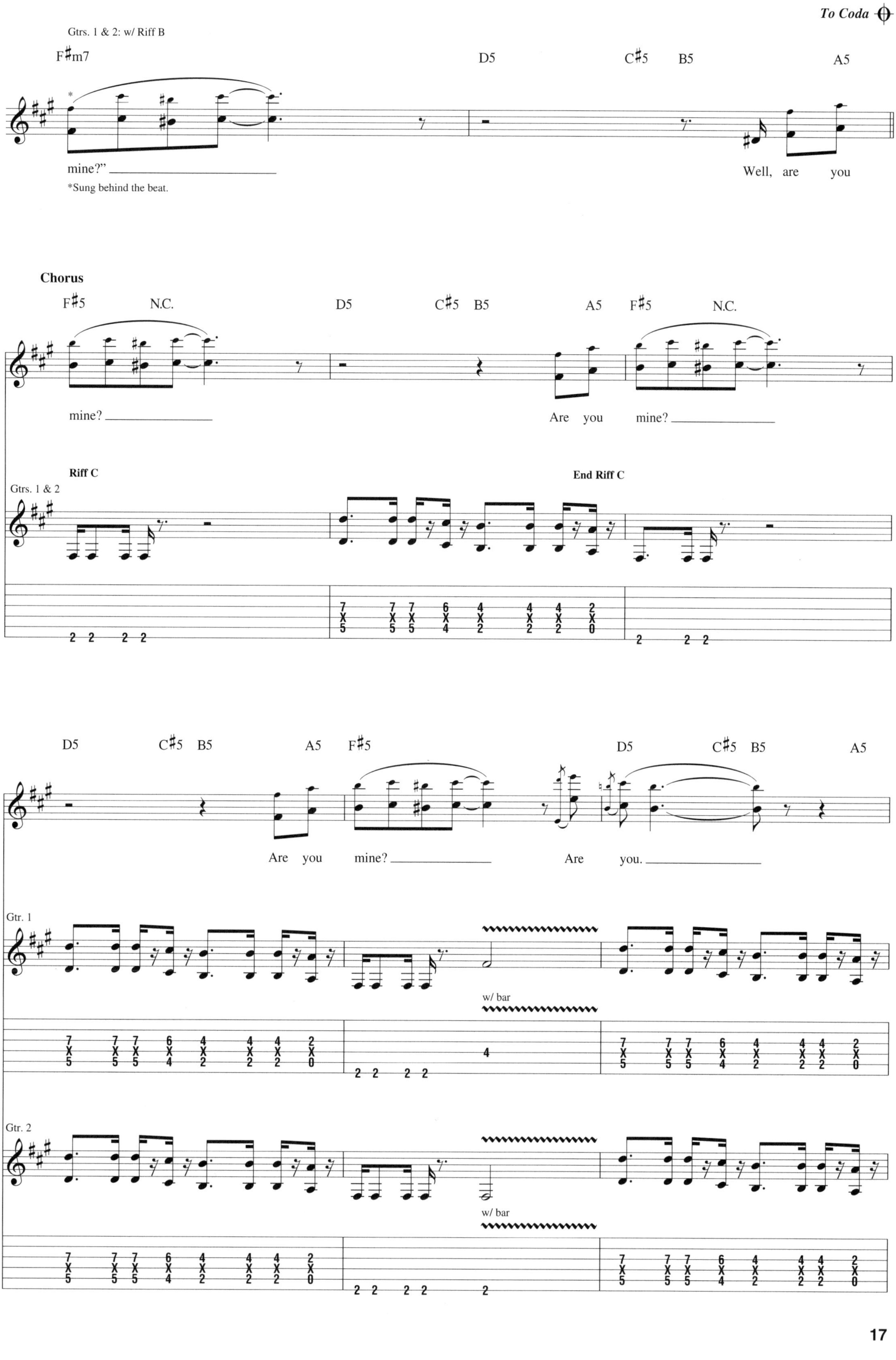

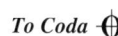

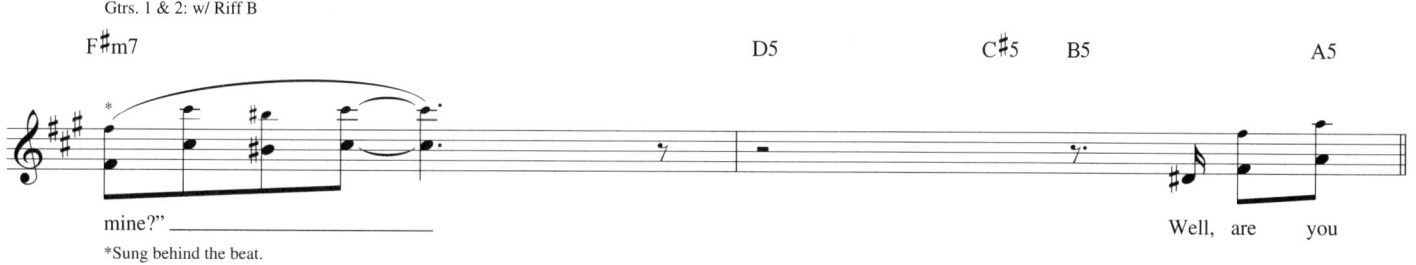

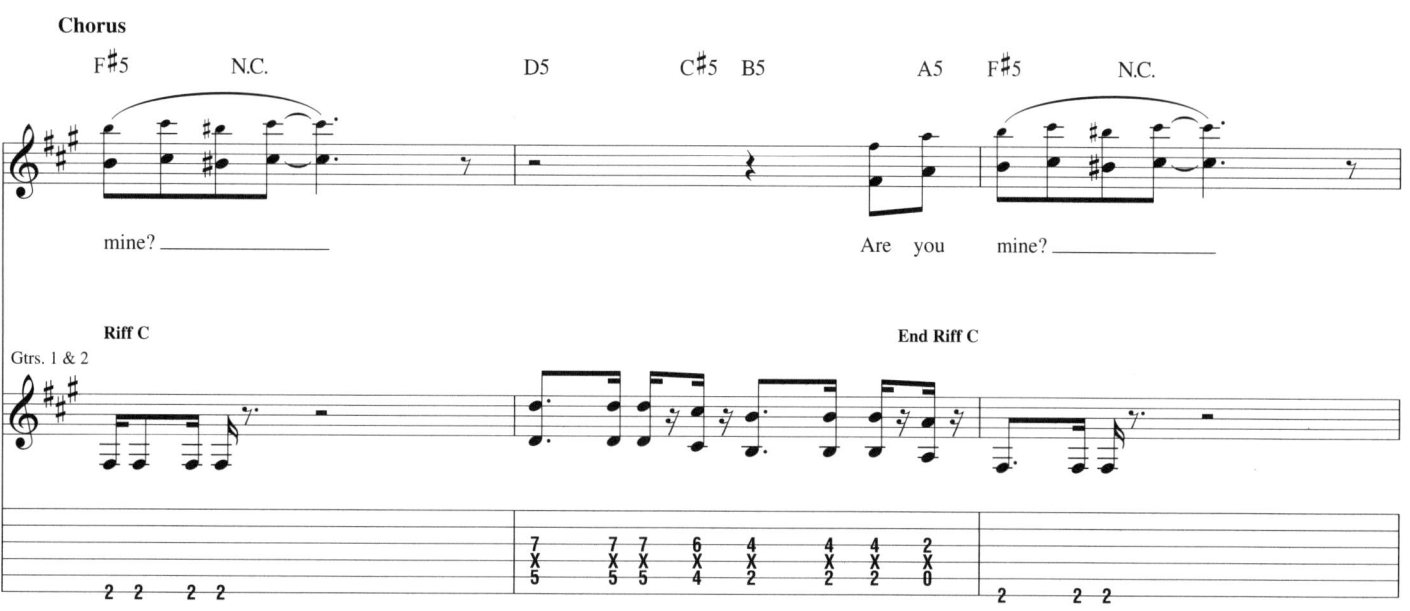

D.S. al Coda
F#5 D5 C#5 B5 A5
time and space. She's a sil - ver lin - ing climb - ing on my de - sire. And
Gtrs. 1 & 2
mf
Gtr. 1, amp tremolo off
Coda
Chorus
N.C. D5 C#5 B5 A5 F#5 N.C.
mine? Are you mine?
Voc. Fig. 1
(R U mine to - mor - row, or just mine
Gtrs. 1 & 2
Gtrs. 1 & 2: w/ Riff C (last meas.)
Gtrs. 1 & 2: w/ Riff C
D5 C#5 B5 A5 F#5 N.C. D5 C#5 B5 A5
Are you mine?
End Voc. Fig. 1
to - night? Are you mine?)

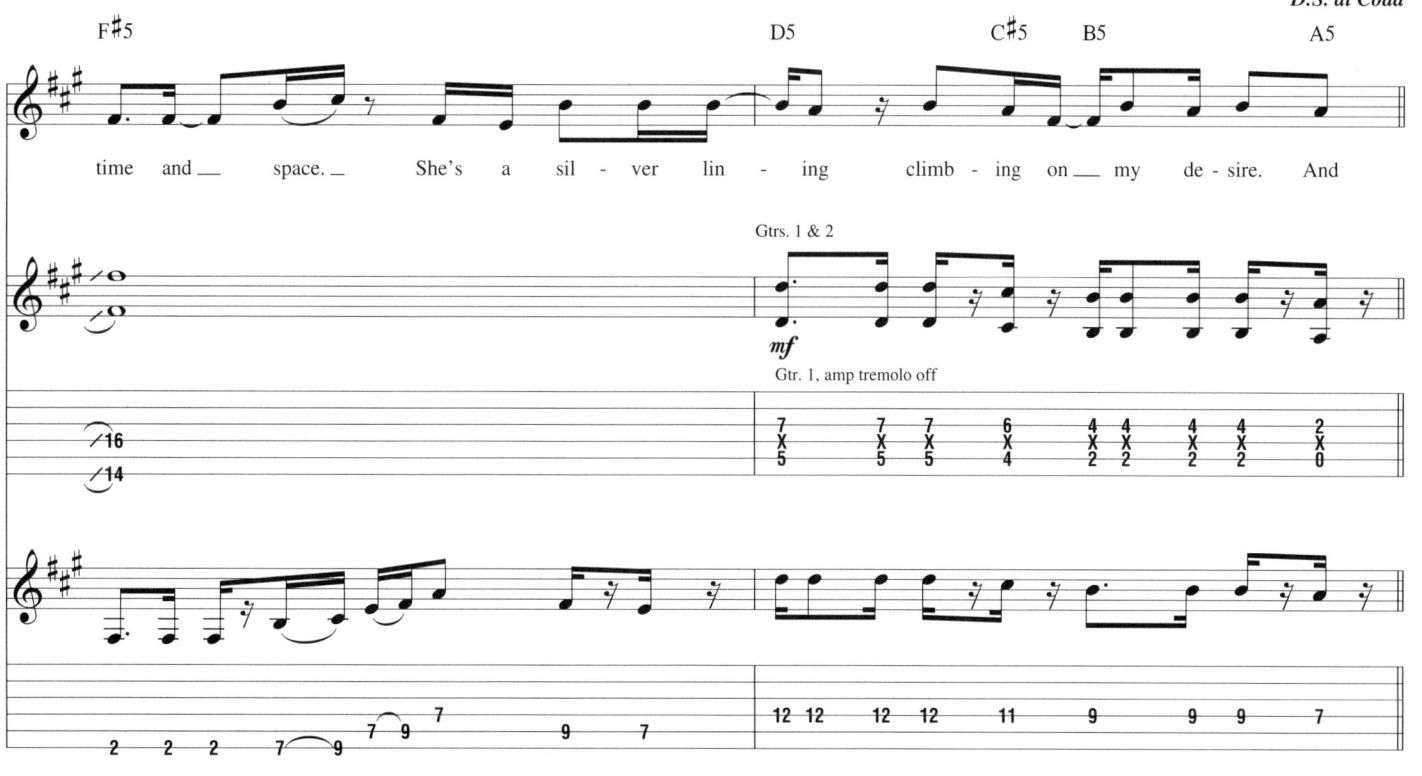

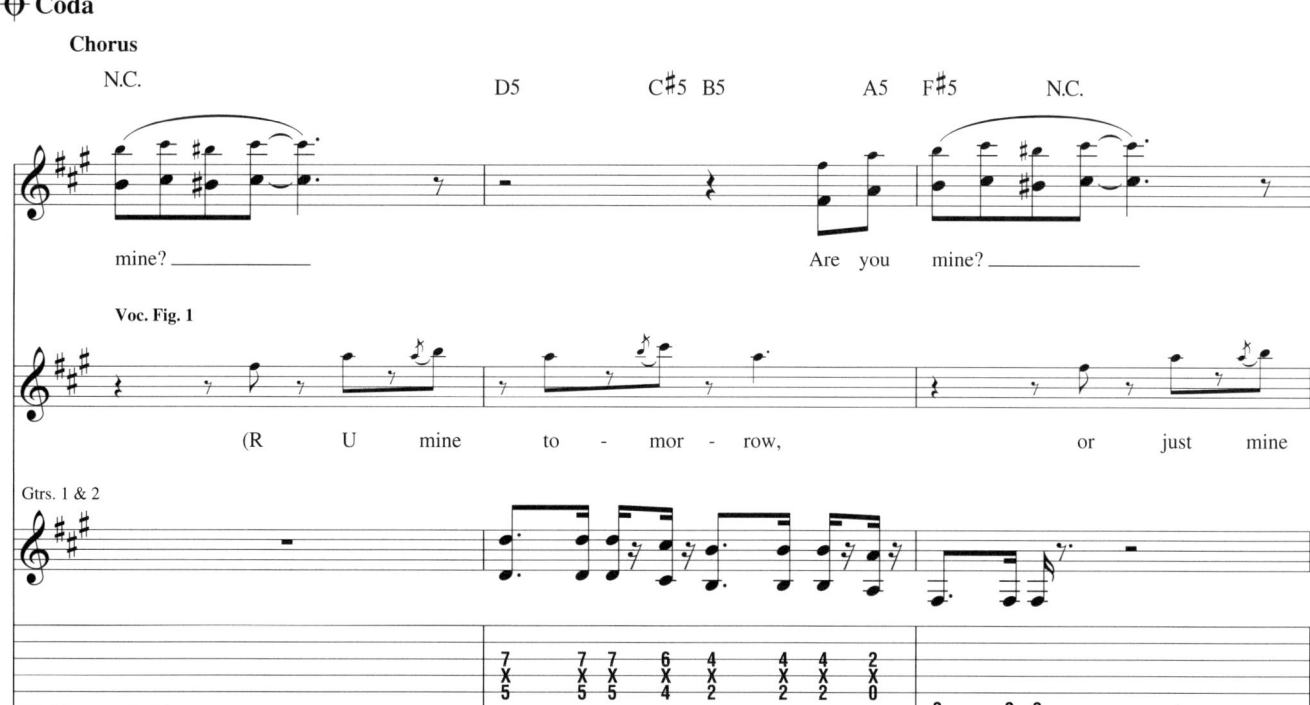

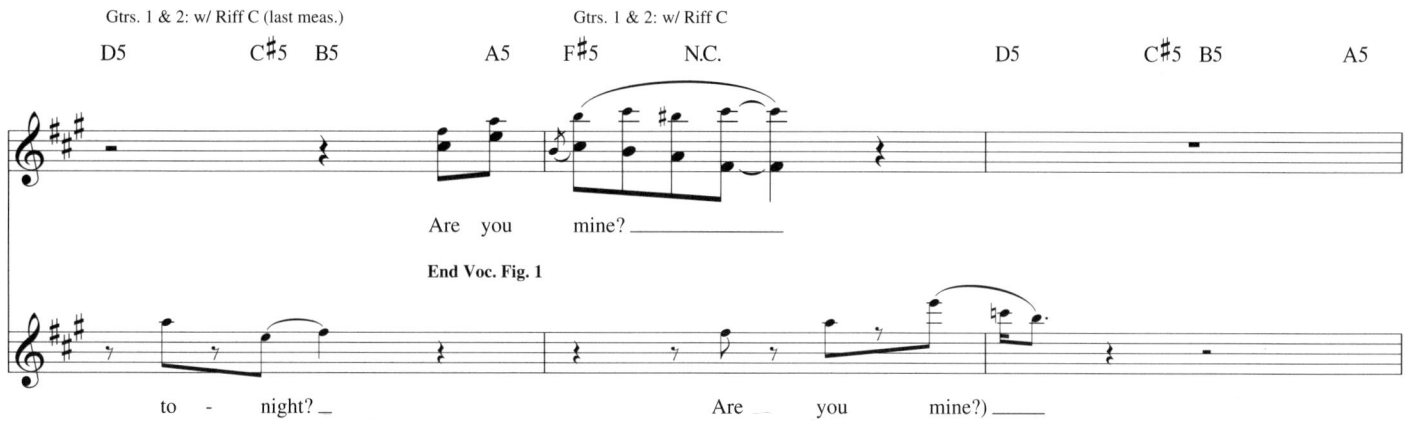

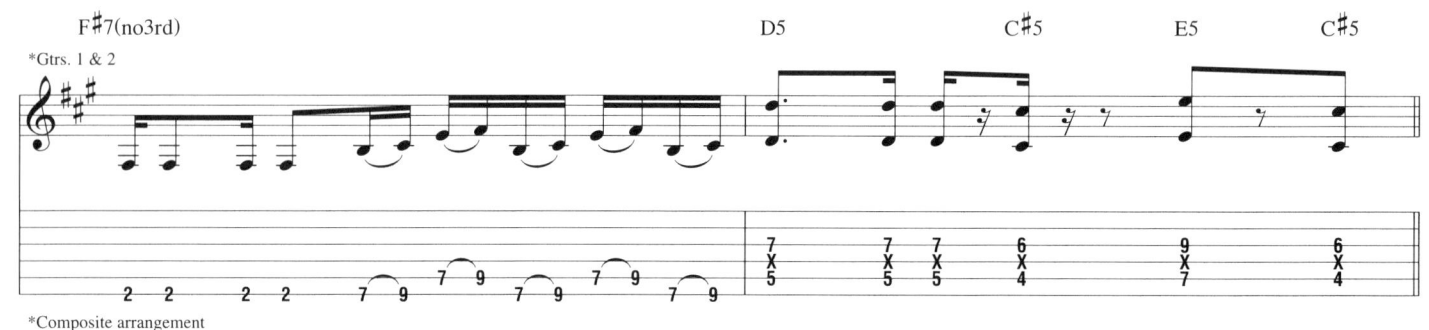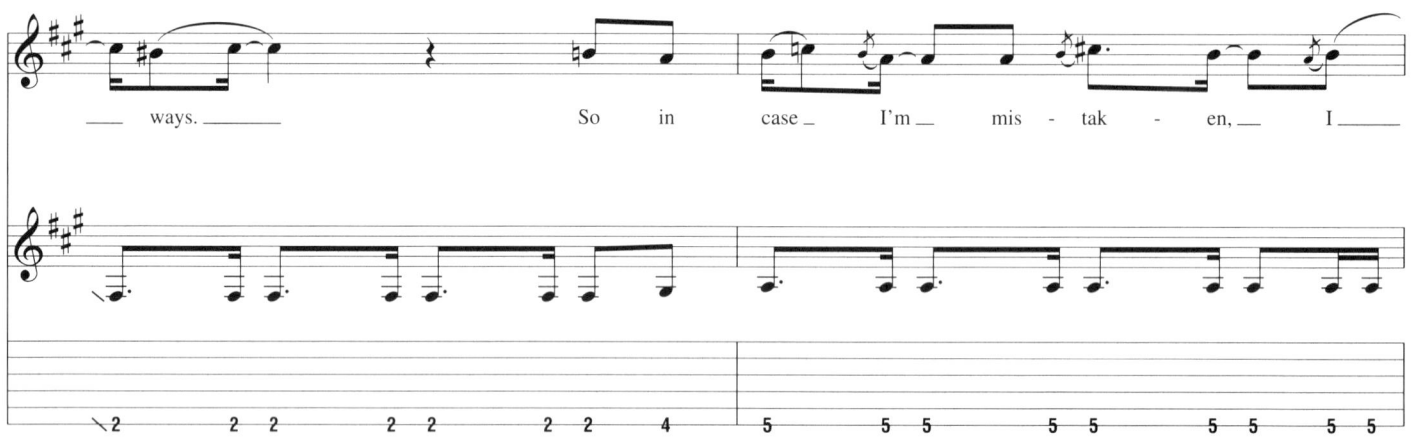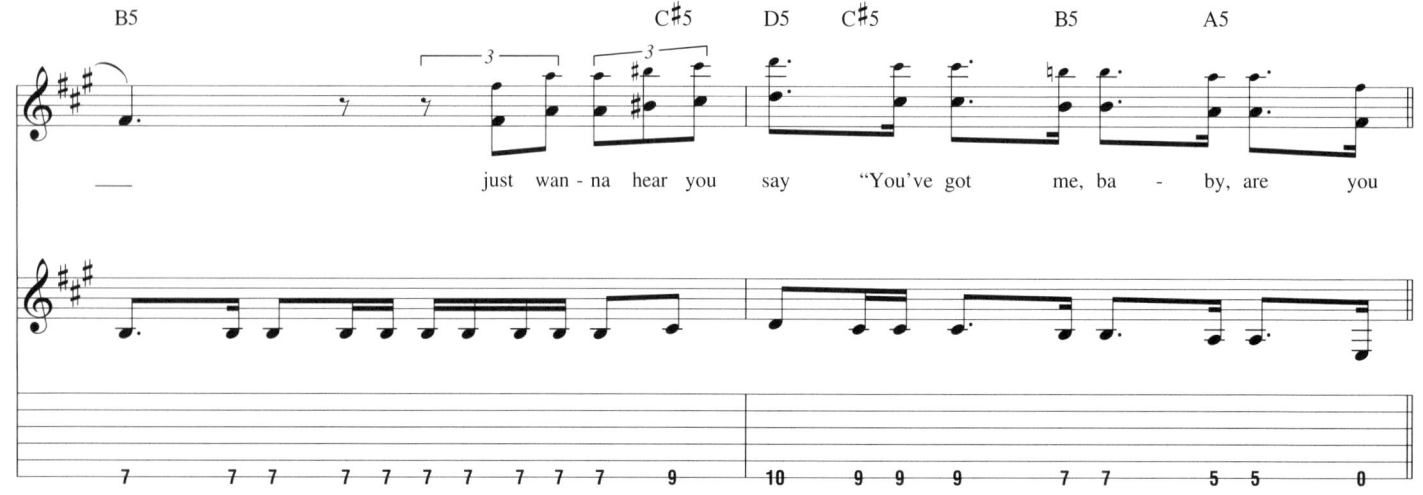

Interlude
Gtr. 1: w/Riff C (1st meas.)
F♯5
N.C.
mine?"
Gtr. 2
Gtr. 2 tacet
F♯5
N.C.
D5
C♯5
B5
C♯5
A5
Gtr. 1
Gtr. 2
tr
Gtr. 3
Verse
Gtrs. 1 & 2: w/ Riff C (1st meas.)
Gtr. 3 tacet
F♯5
N.C.
3. She's a sil - ver lin - ing, lone rang - er rid - ing through an o - pen space in my mind.
Gtr. 3

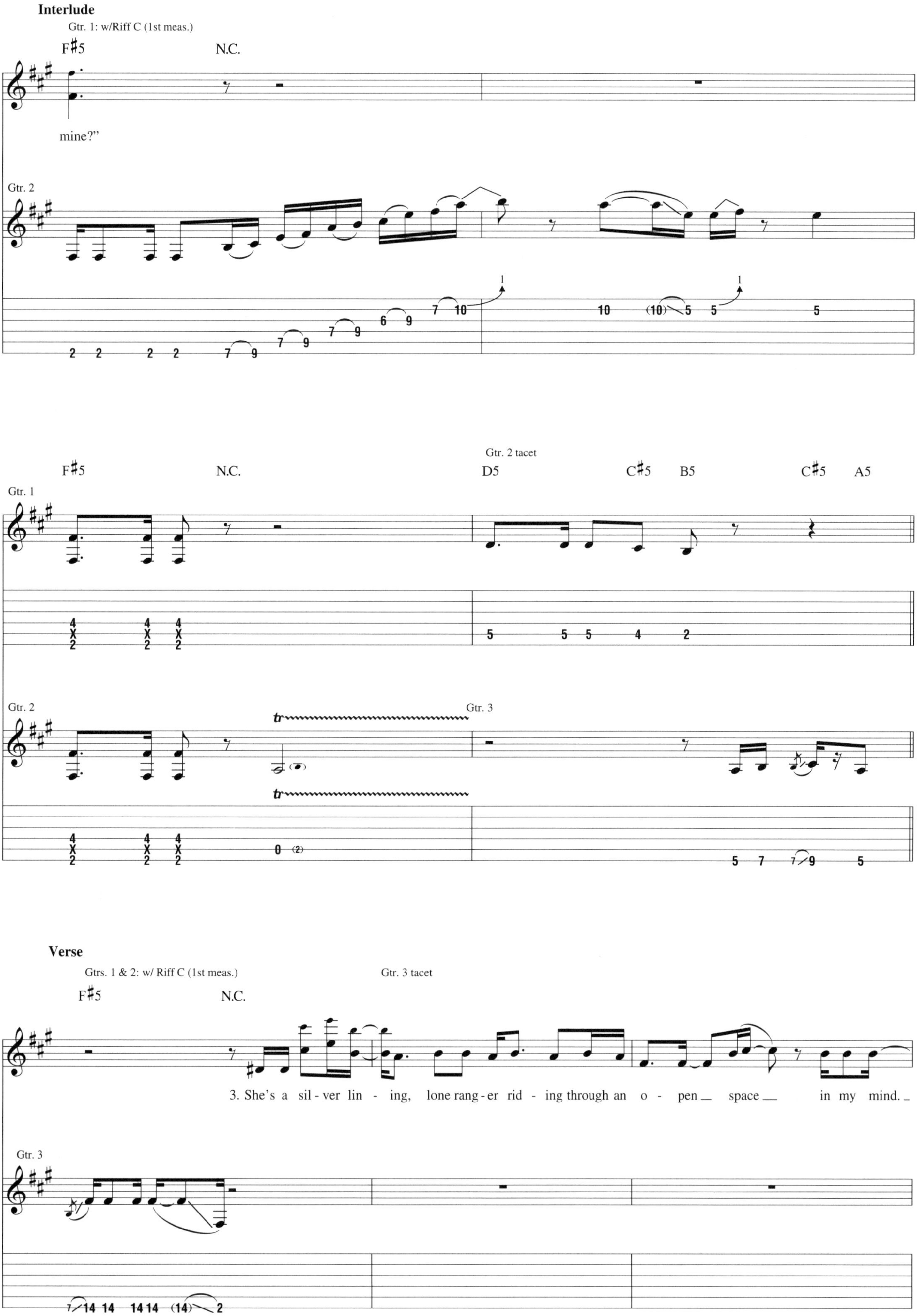

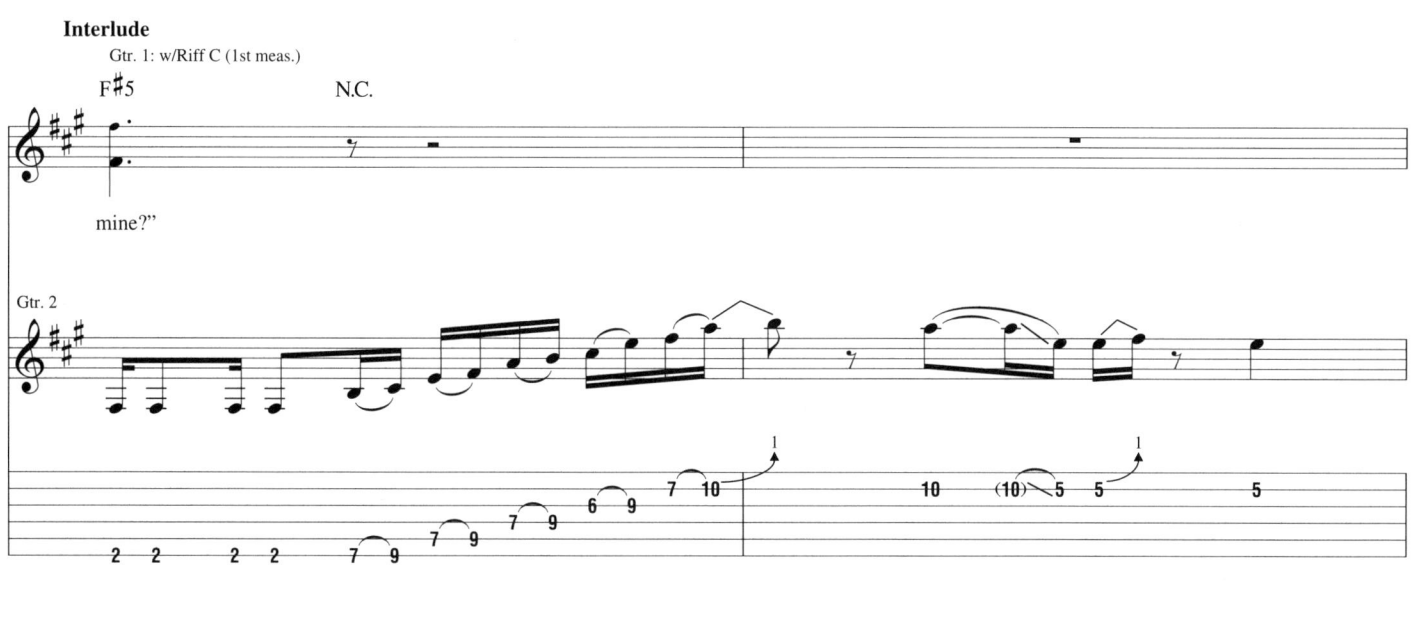

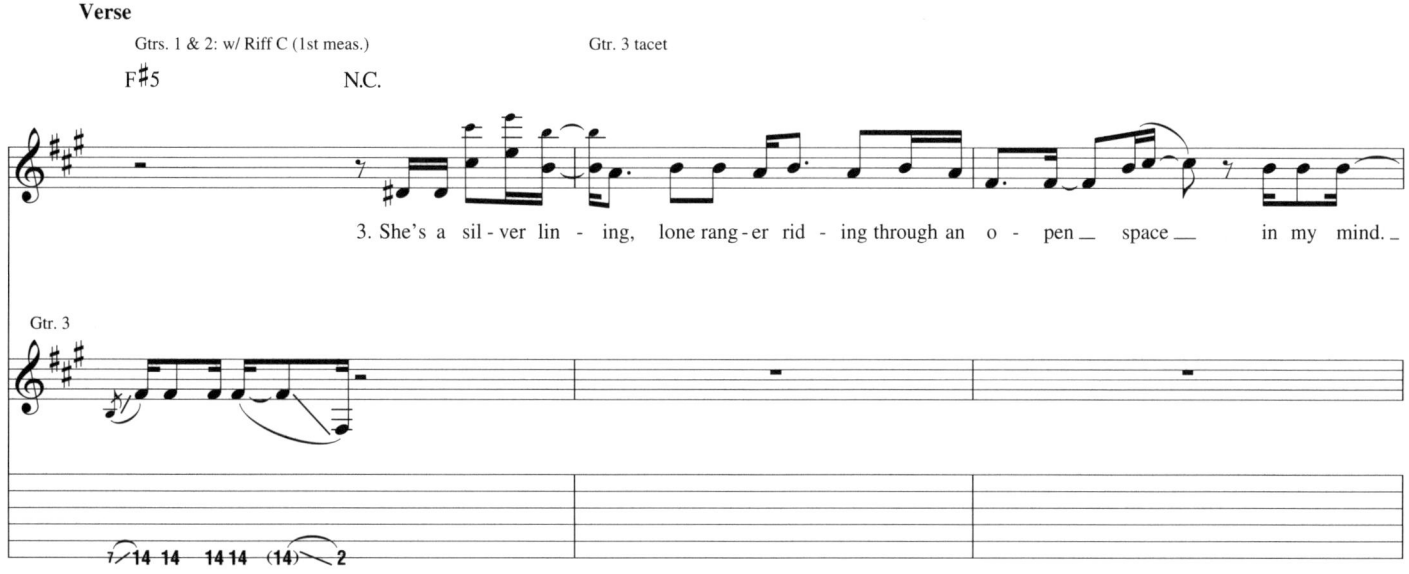

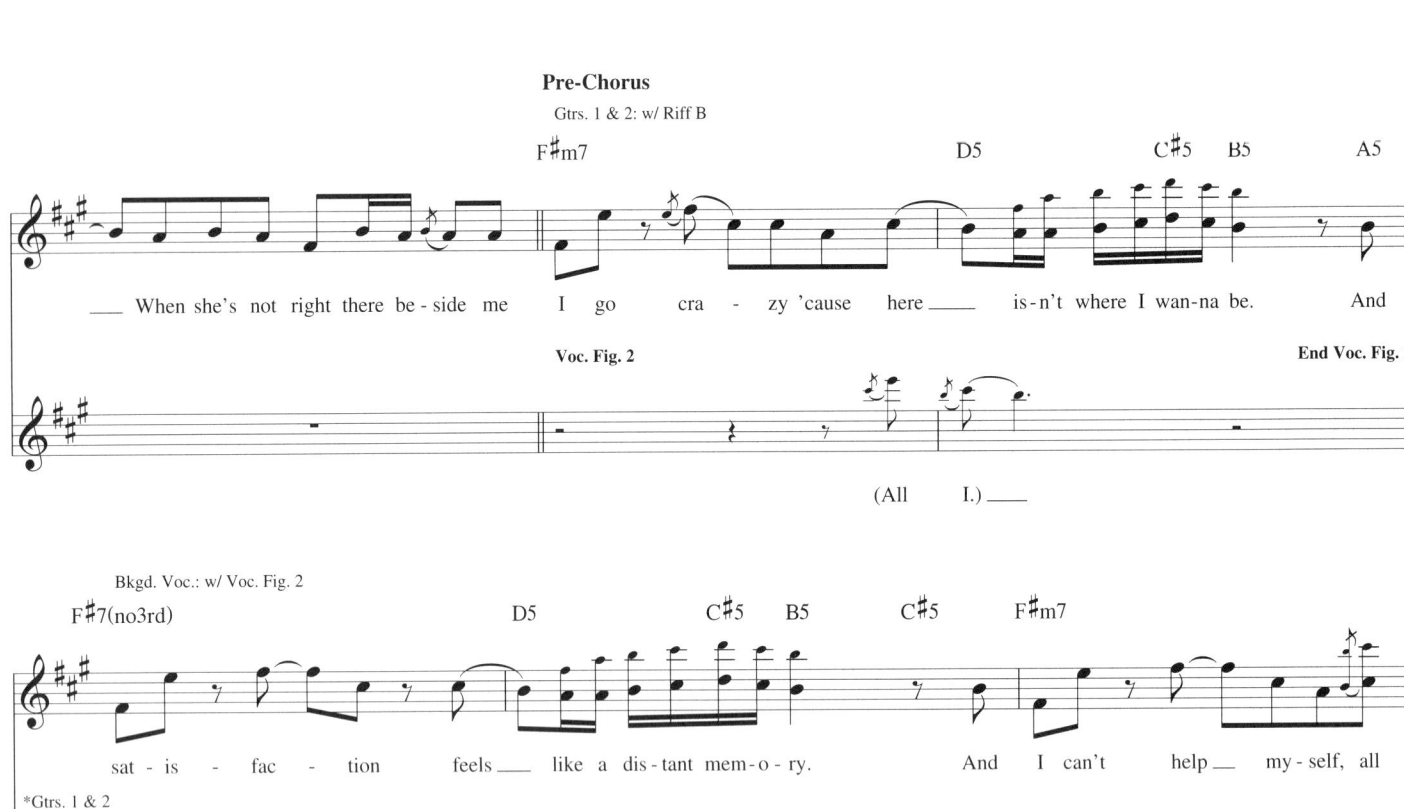
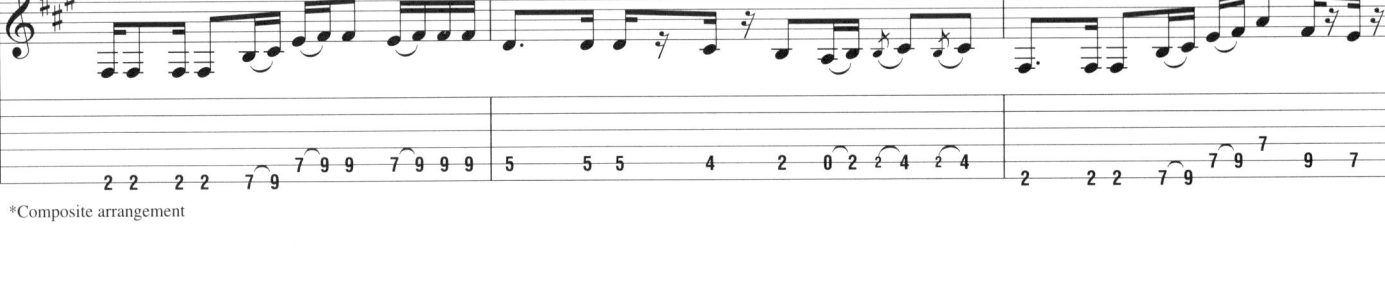

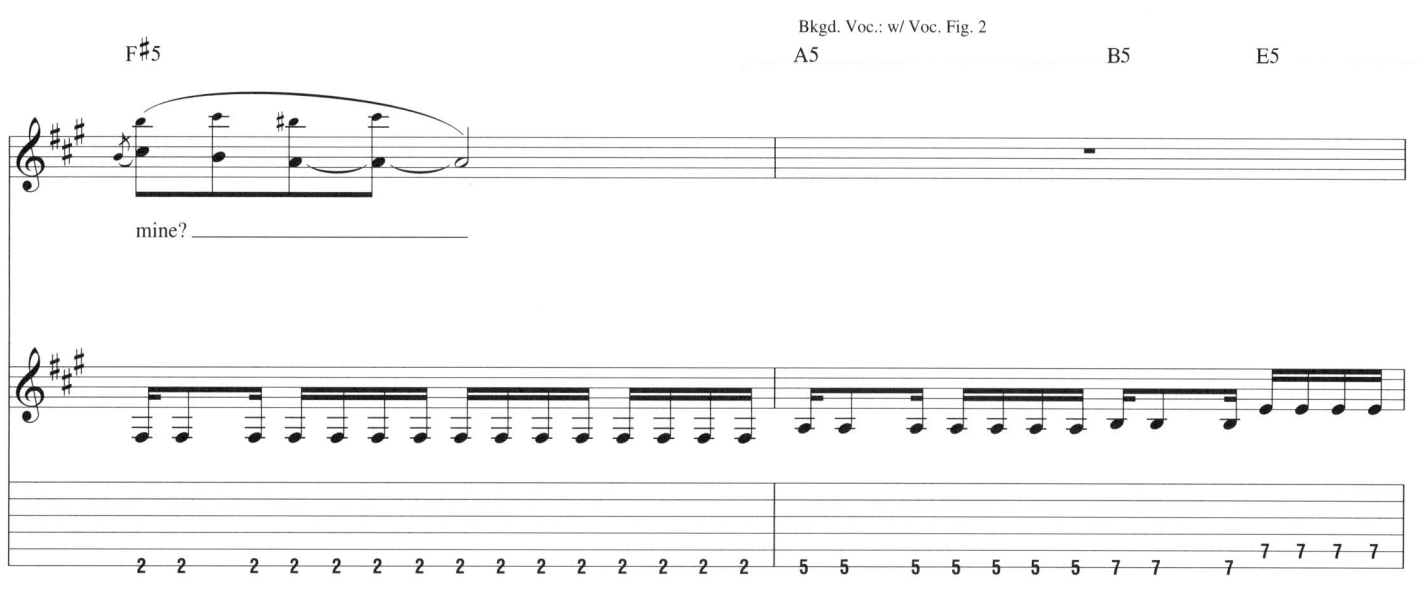

One for the Road

Words by Alex Turner
Music by Arctic Monkeys

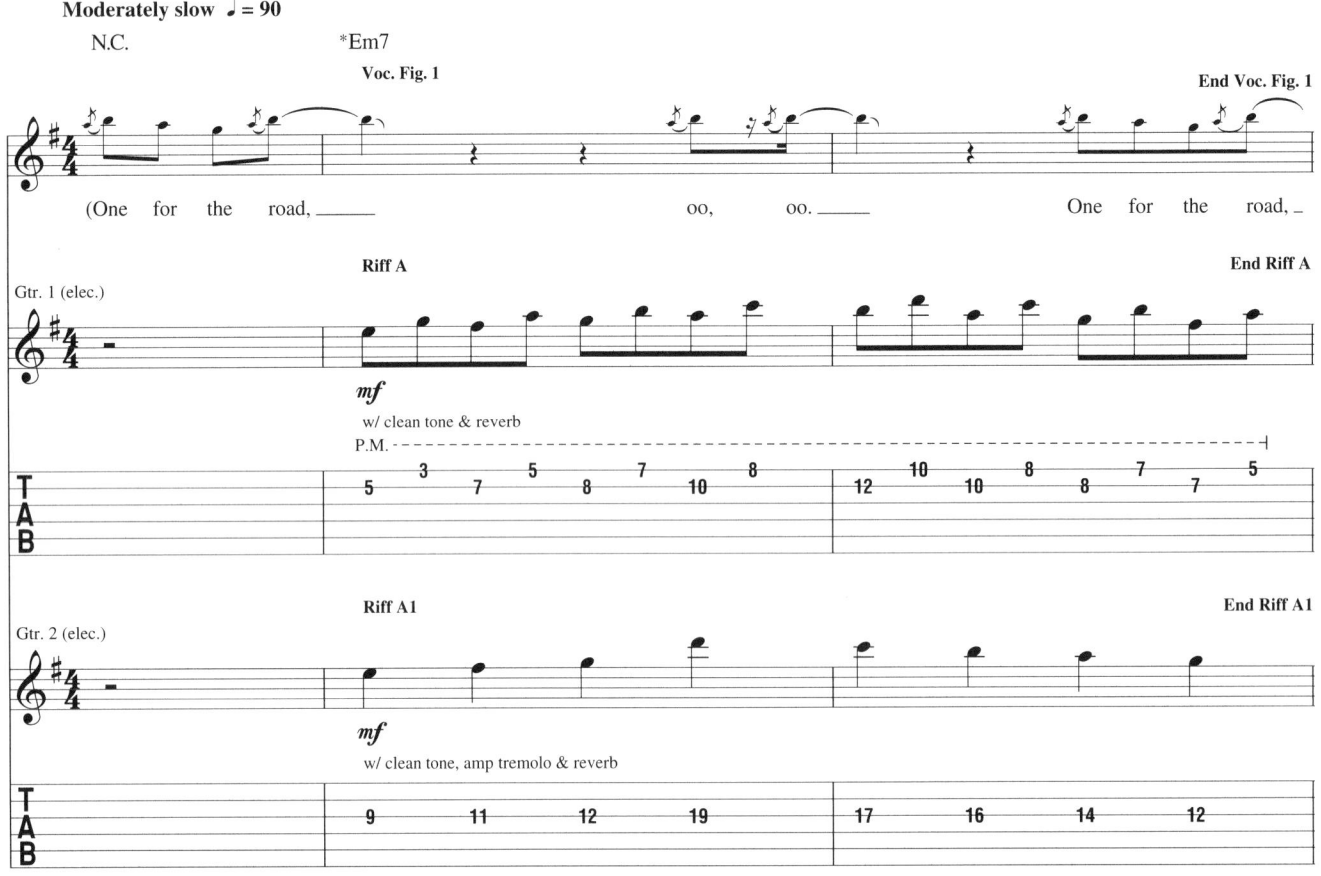

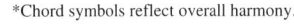
*Chord symbols reflect overall harmony.

**Two gtrs. arr. for one.

© 2013 EMI MUSIC PUBLISHING LTD.
All Rights in the U.S. and Canada Controlled and Administered by EMI APRIL MUSIC INC.
All Rights Reserved   International Copyright Secured   Used by Permission

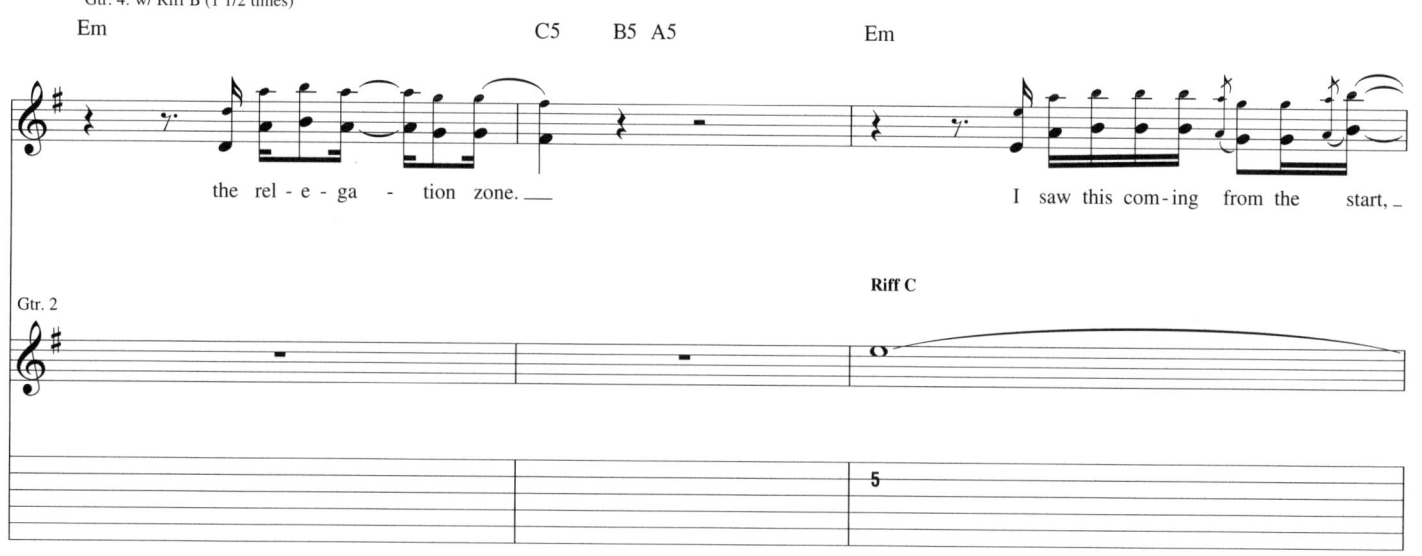

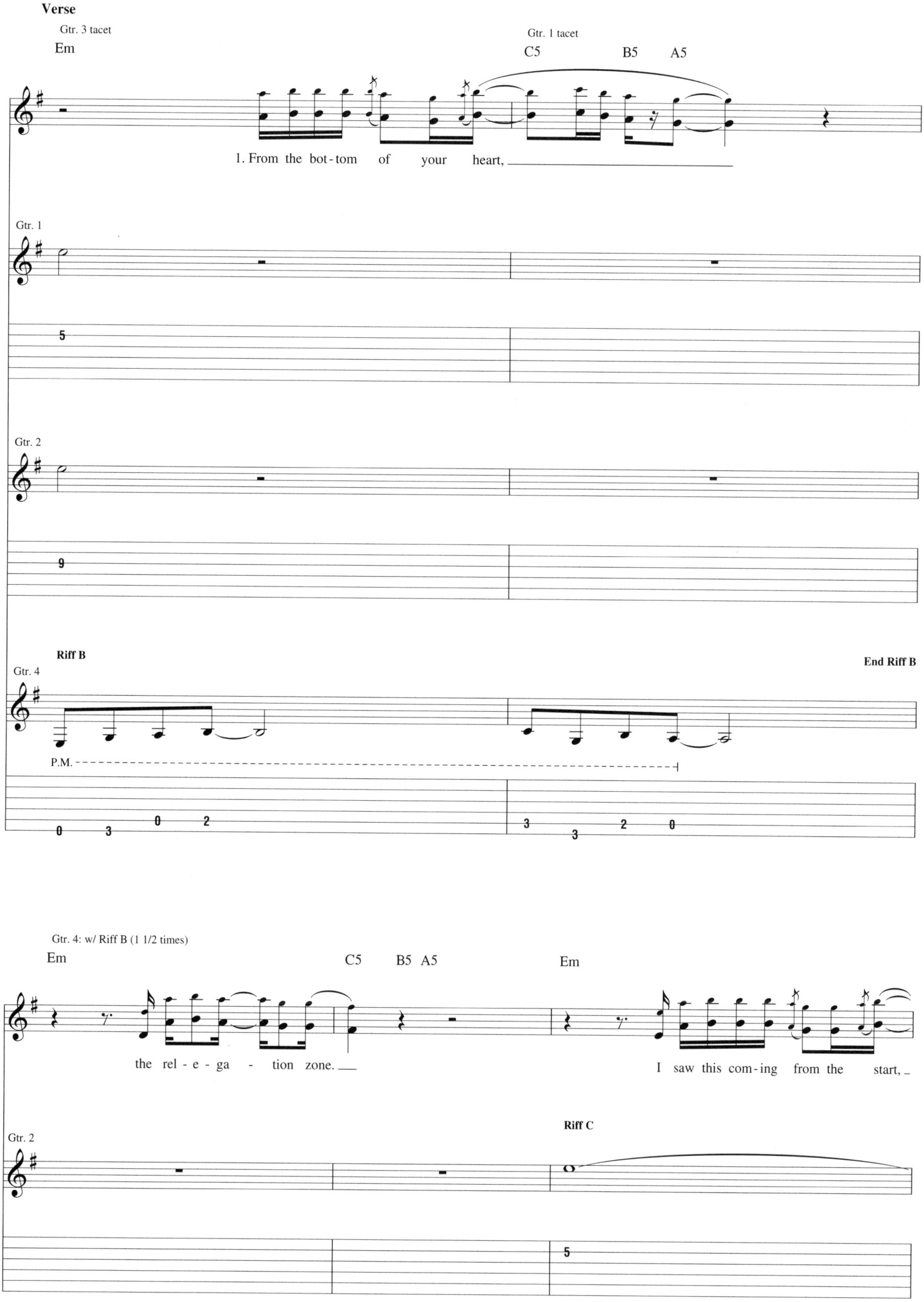
Verse
Gtr. 3 tacet
Em
Gtr. 1 tacet
C5 B5 A5
1. From the bot-tom of your heart,
Gtr. 1
5
Gtr. 2
9
Riff B
End Riff B
Gtr. 4
P.M.
0 3 0 2
3 3 2 0
Gtr. 4: w/ Riff B (1 1/2 times)
Em
C5 B5 A5
Em
the rel - e - ga - tion zone.
I saw this com-ing from the start,
Riff C
Gtr. 2
5

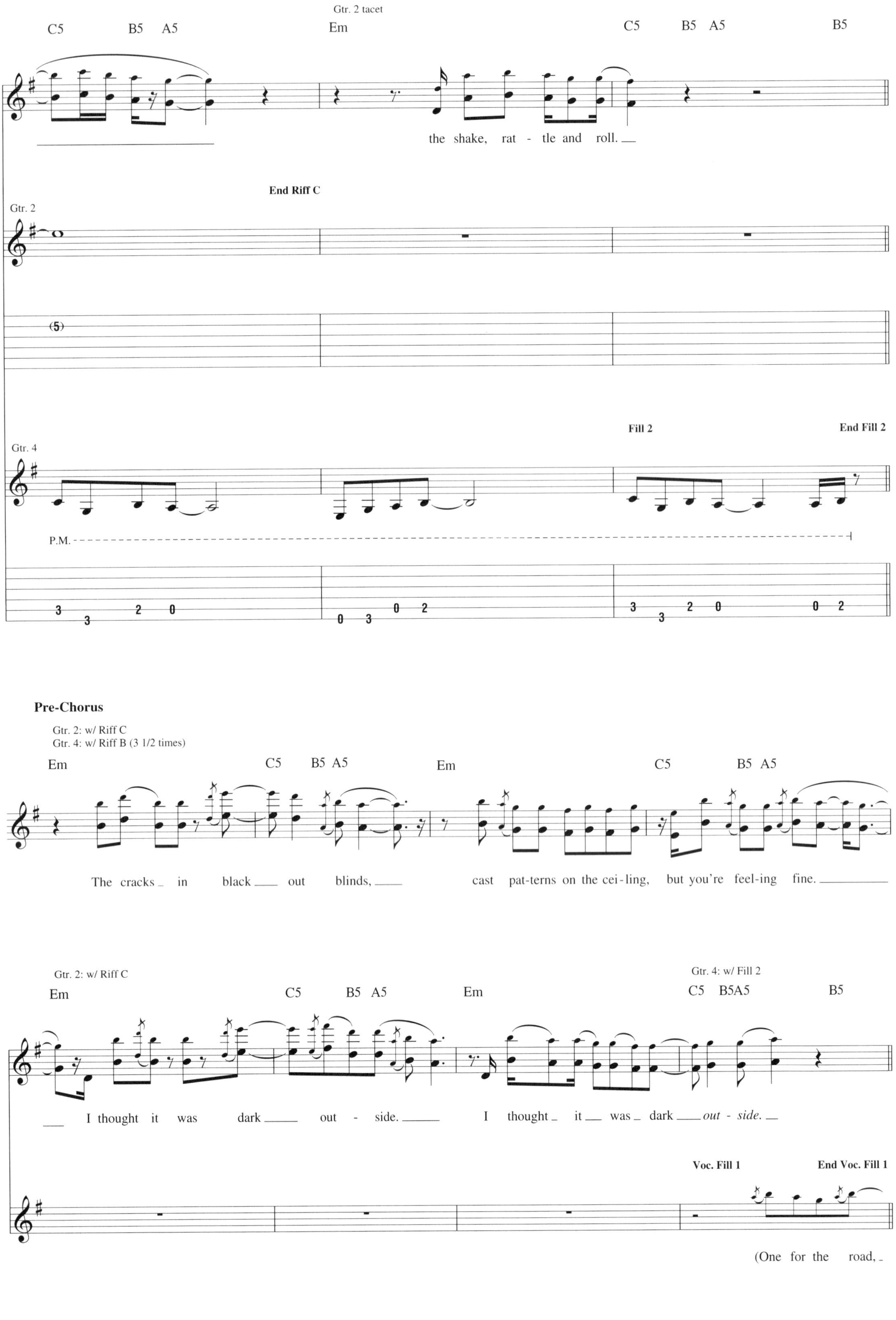
Gtr. 2 tacet
C5 B5 A5 Em C5 B5 A5 B5
the shake, rat - tle and roll.
End Riff C
Gtr. 2
(5)
Fill 2
End Fill 2
Gtr. 4
P.M.
3 3 2 0 0 3 0 2 3 3 2 0 0 2
Pre-Chorus
Gtr. 2: w/ Riff C
Gtr. 4: w/ Riff B (3 1/2 times)
Em C5 B5 A5 Em C5 B5 A5
The cracks in black out blinds, cast pat-terns on the cei-ling, but you're feel-ing fine.
Gtr. 2: w/ Riff C
Gtr. 4: w/ Fill 2
Em C5 B5 A5 Em C5 B5A5 B5
I thought it was dark out - side. I thought it was dark out - side.
Voc. Fill 1
End Voc. Fill 1
(One for the road,

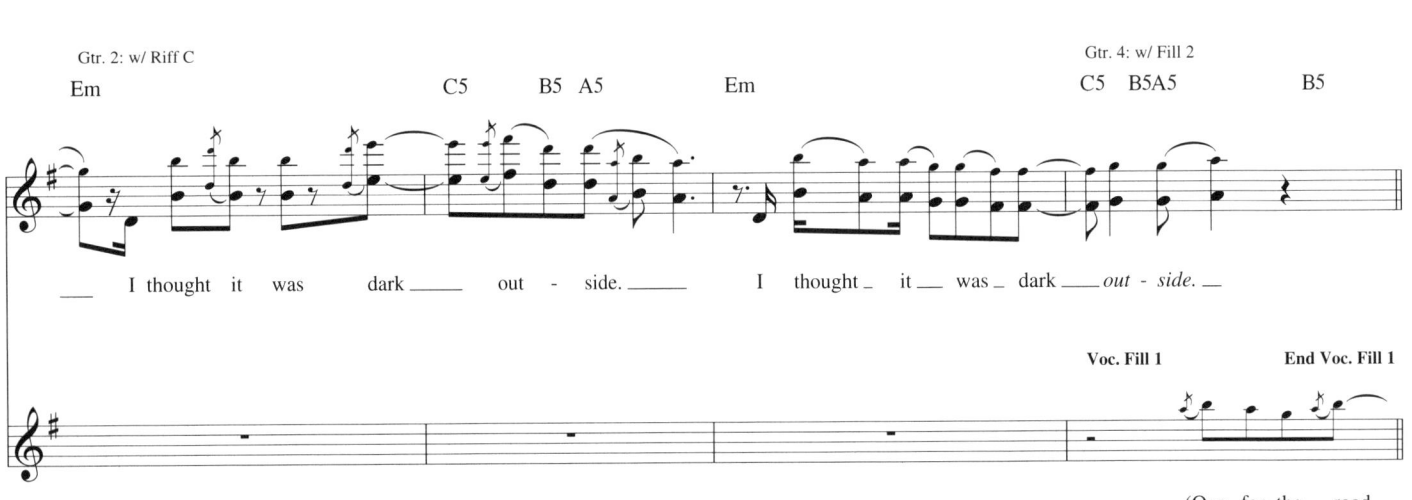

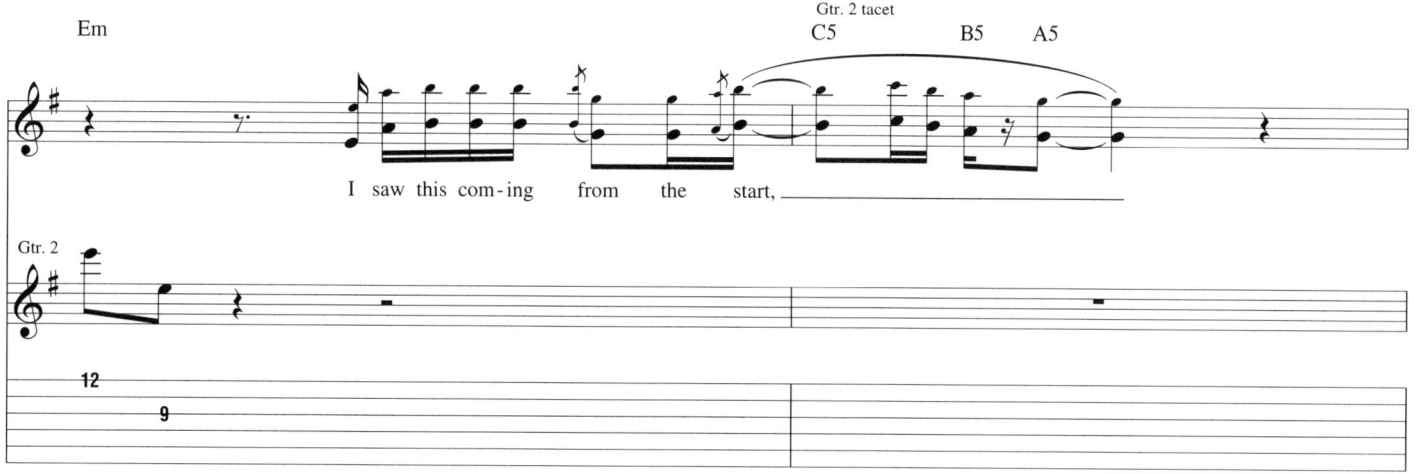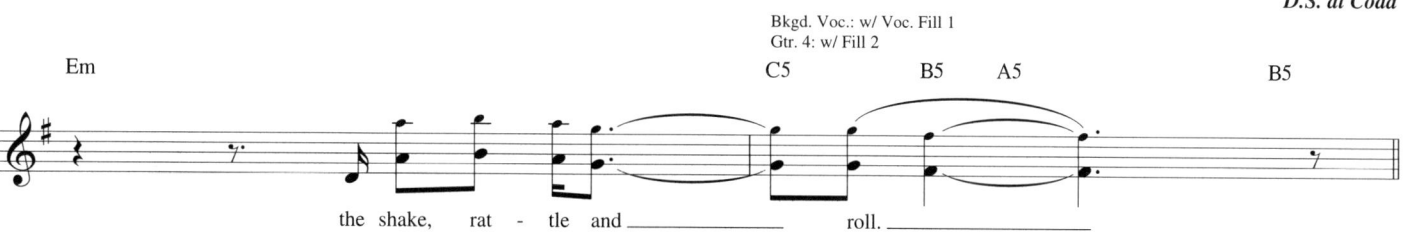

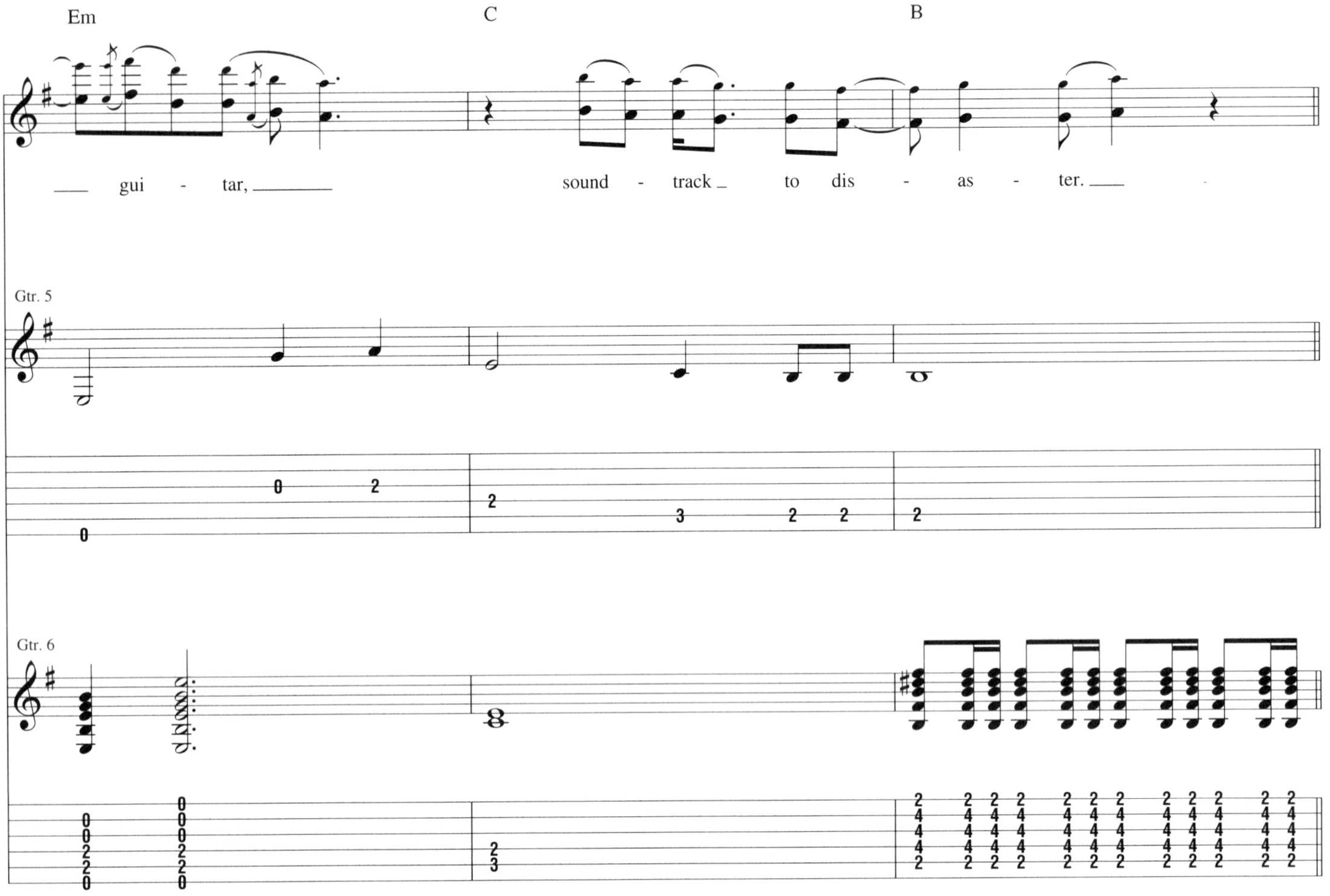

Interlude

Gtr. 1: w/ Riff A (4 times)
Gtr. 2: w/ Riff C
Gtrs. 5 & 6 tacet

*Doubled throughout

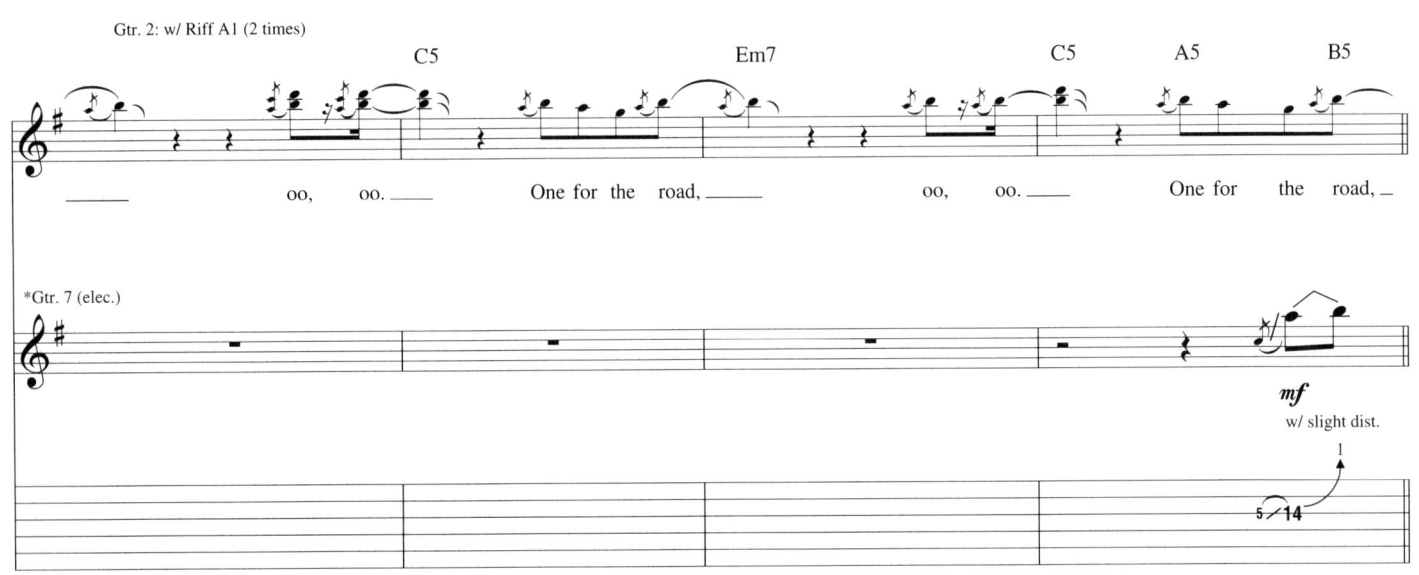

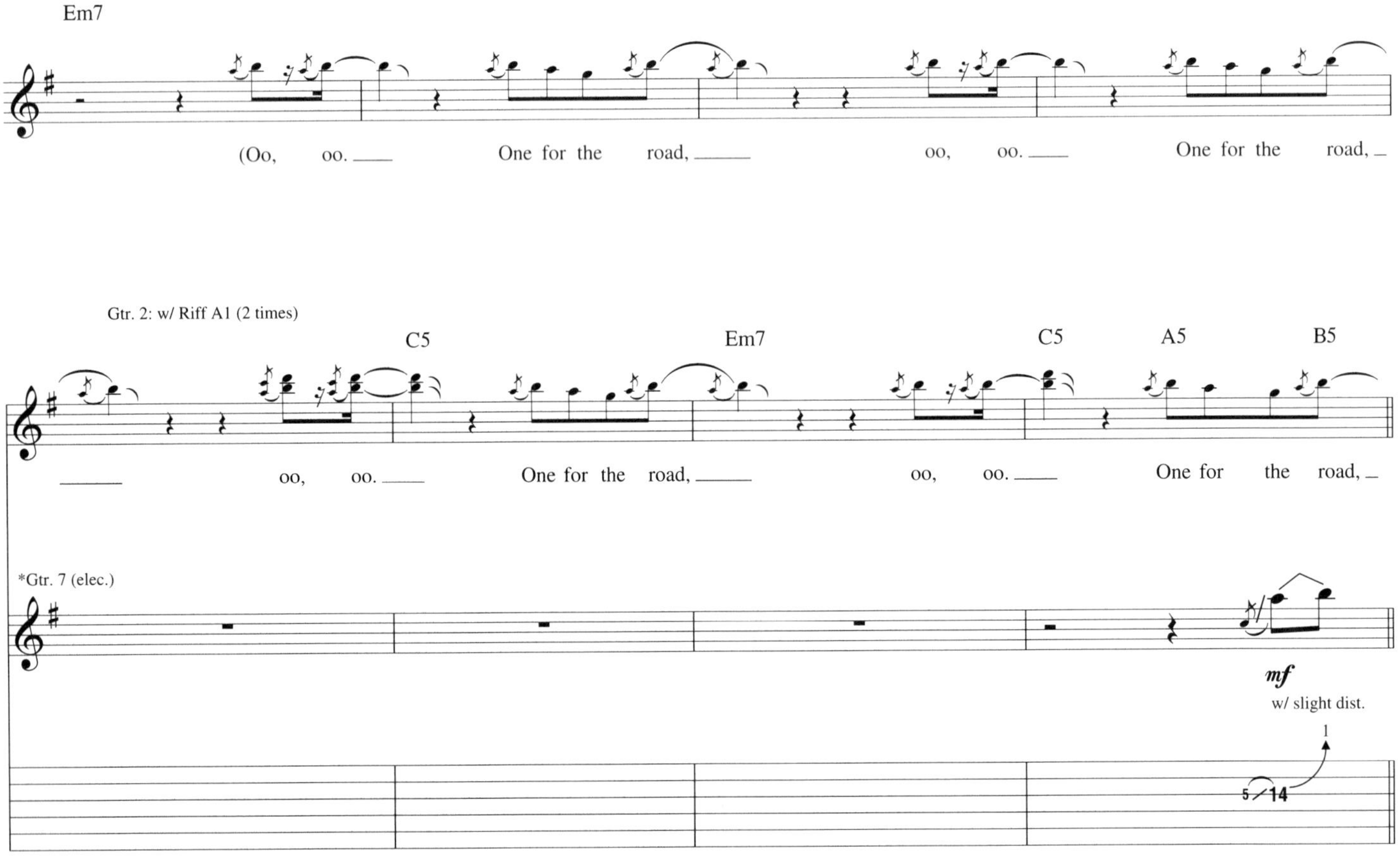

Guitar Solo

C
Em
oo,
oo.
Gtr. 7
Riff G
End Riff G
Gtr. 5
Gtr. 5: w/ Riff G (3 times)
C
Em
Oo,
oo.
Gtr. 7
C
Em
Oo,
oo.

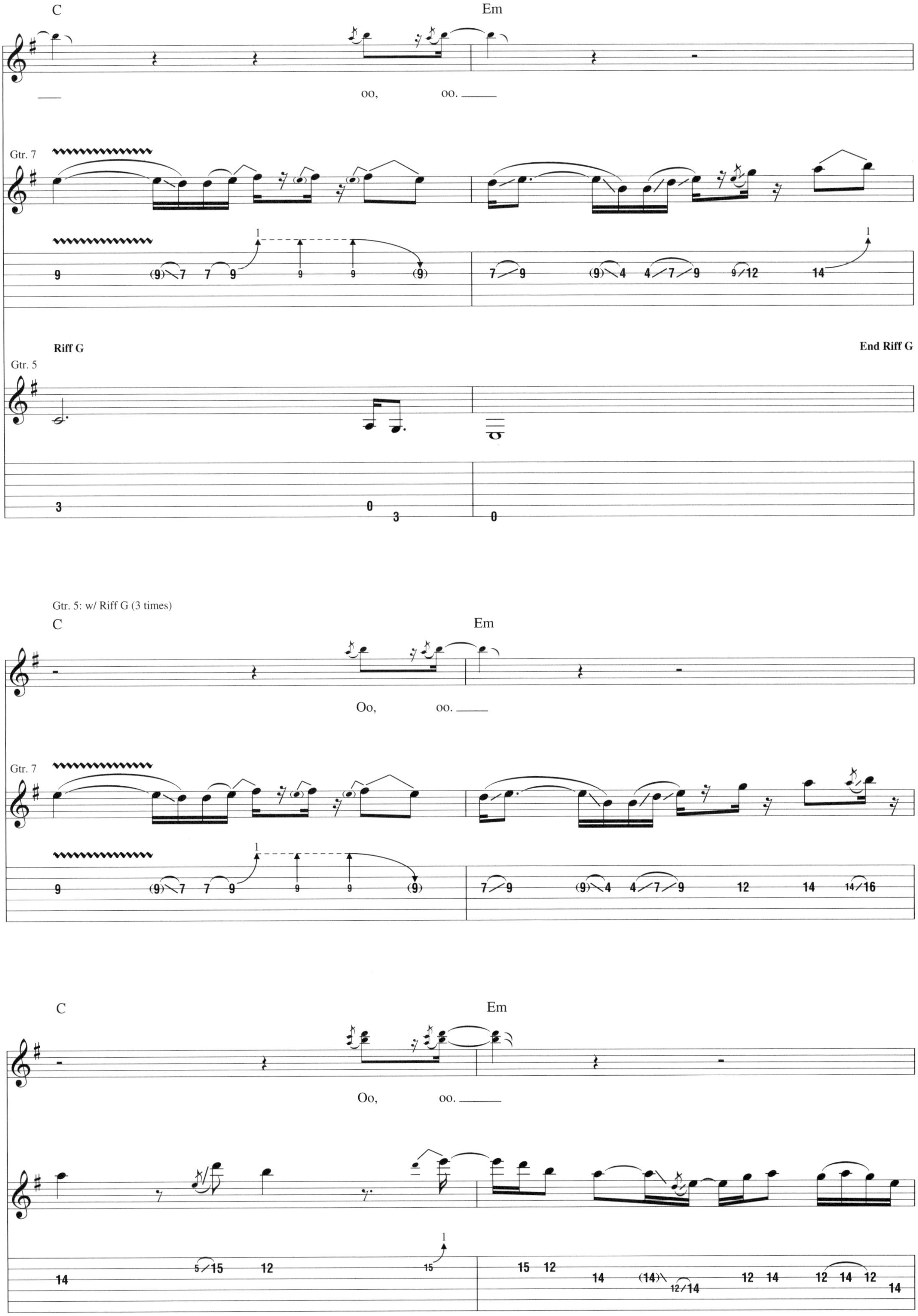

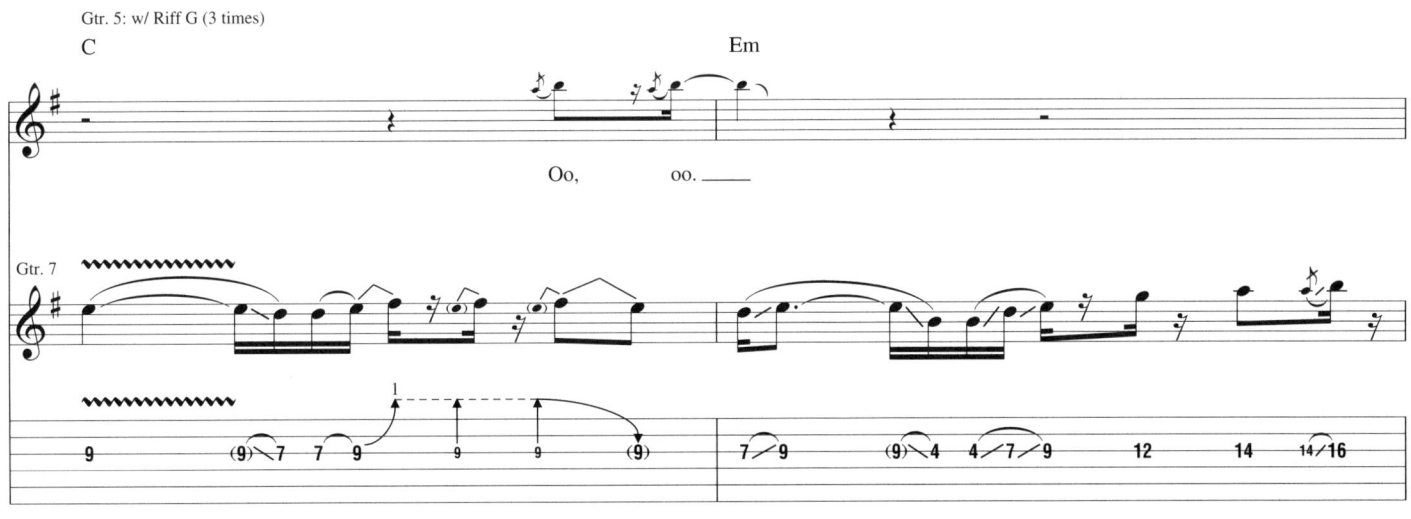

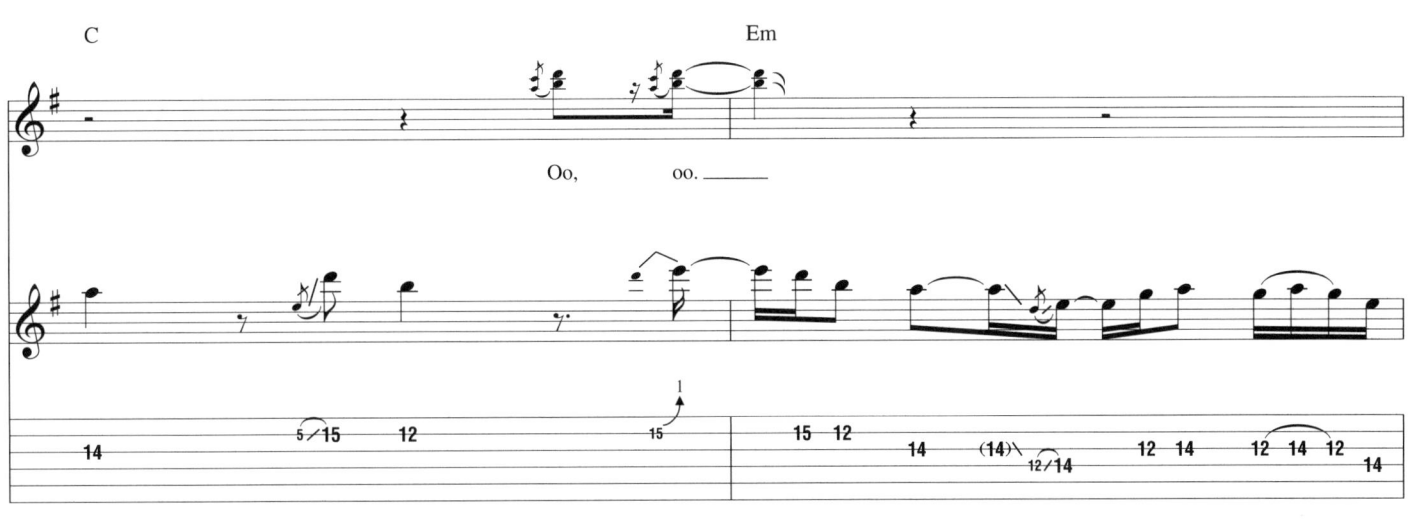

Arabella

Words by Alex Turner
Music by Arctic Monkeys

Gtrs. 2-9: Drop D tuning:
(low to high) D-A-D-G-B-E

Intro
Moderately slow ♩ = 92

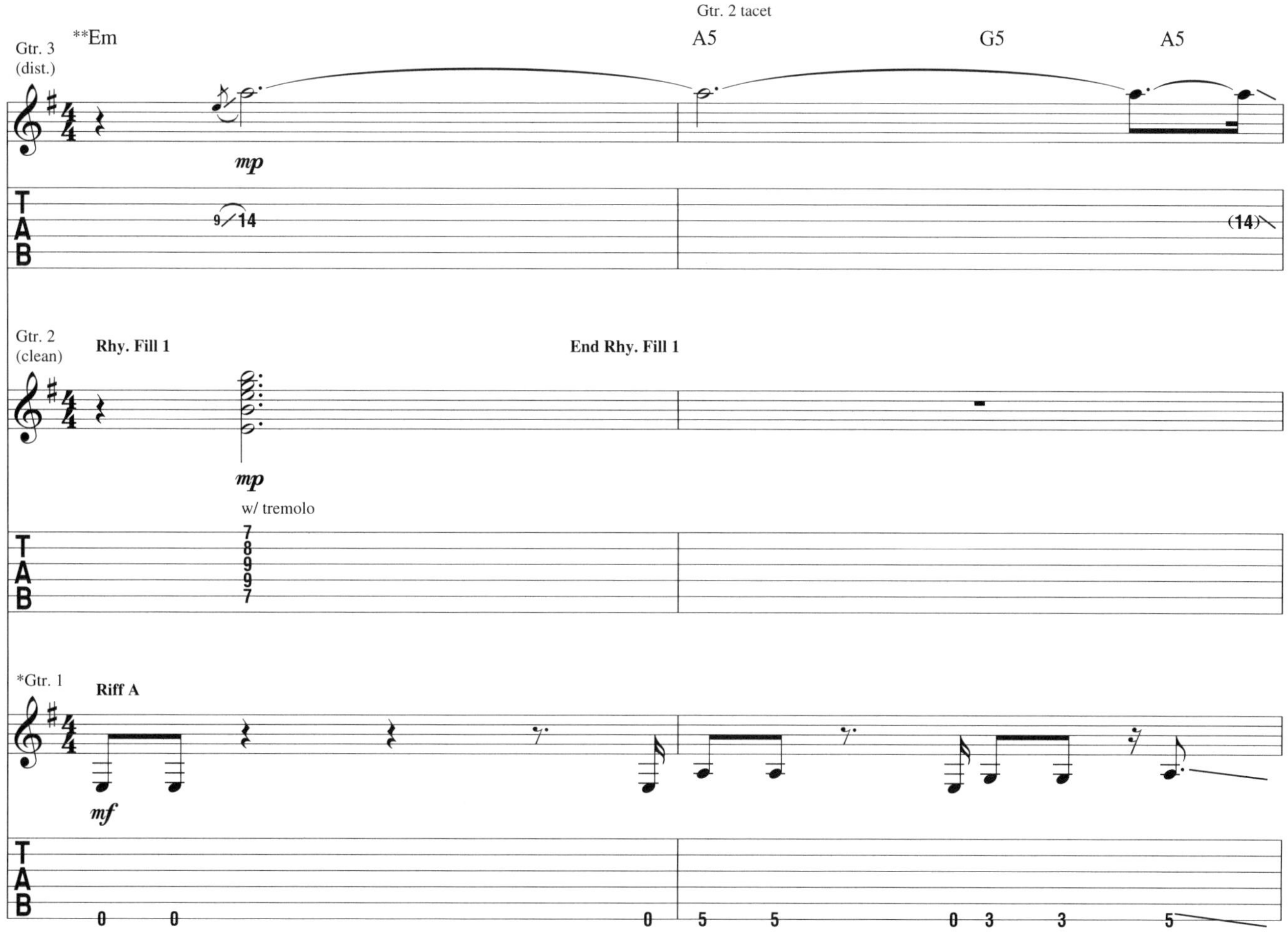

*Bass arr. for gtr.
**Chord symbols reflect implied harmony.

***Doubled throughout

†Vol. swell

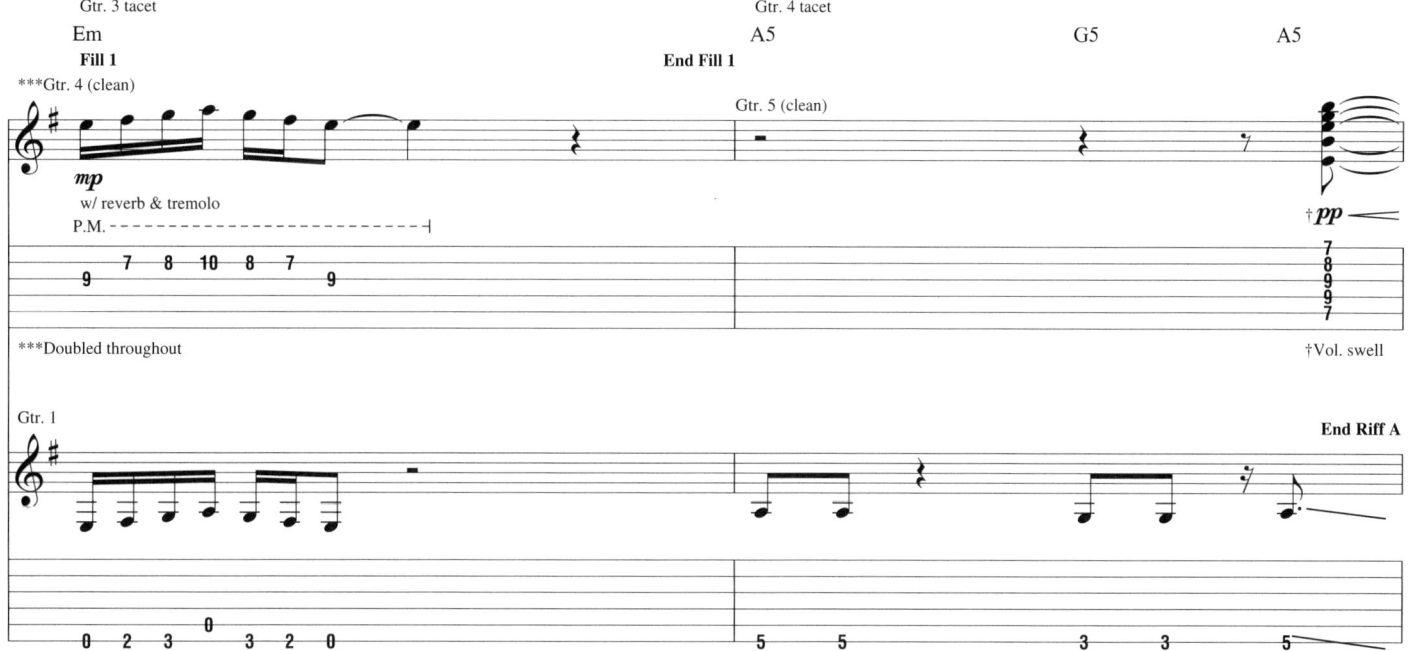

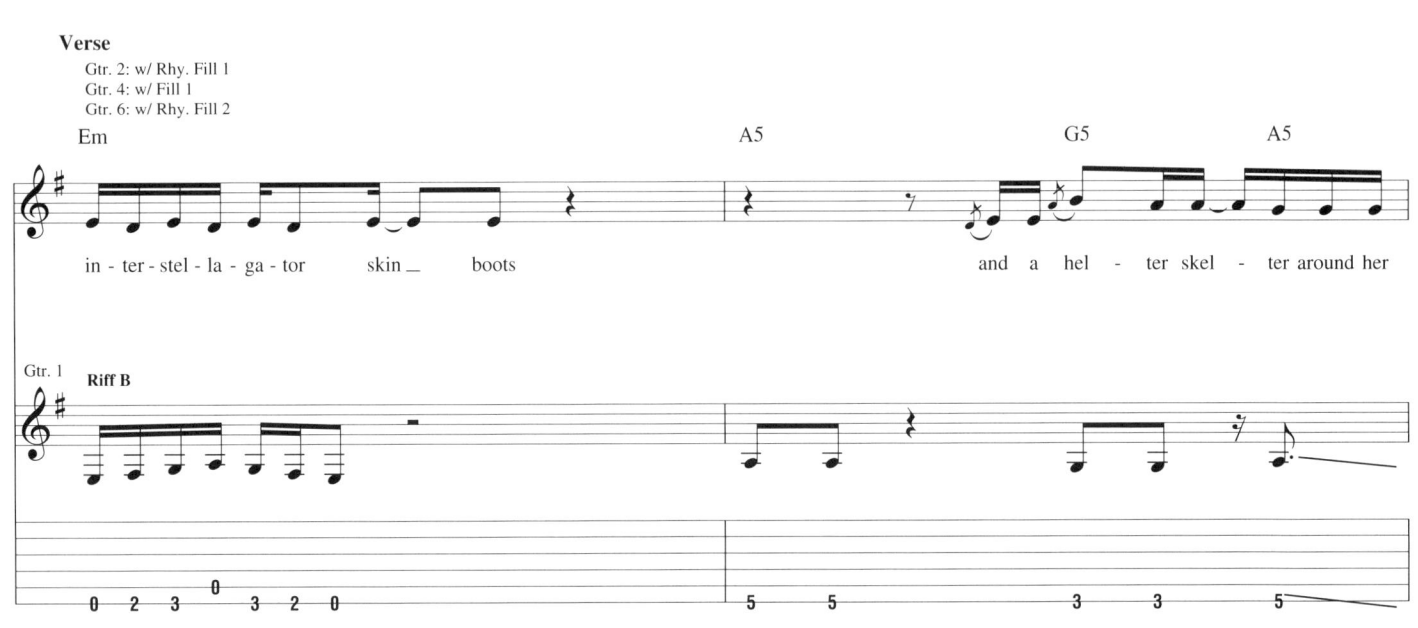

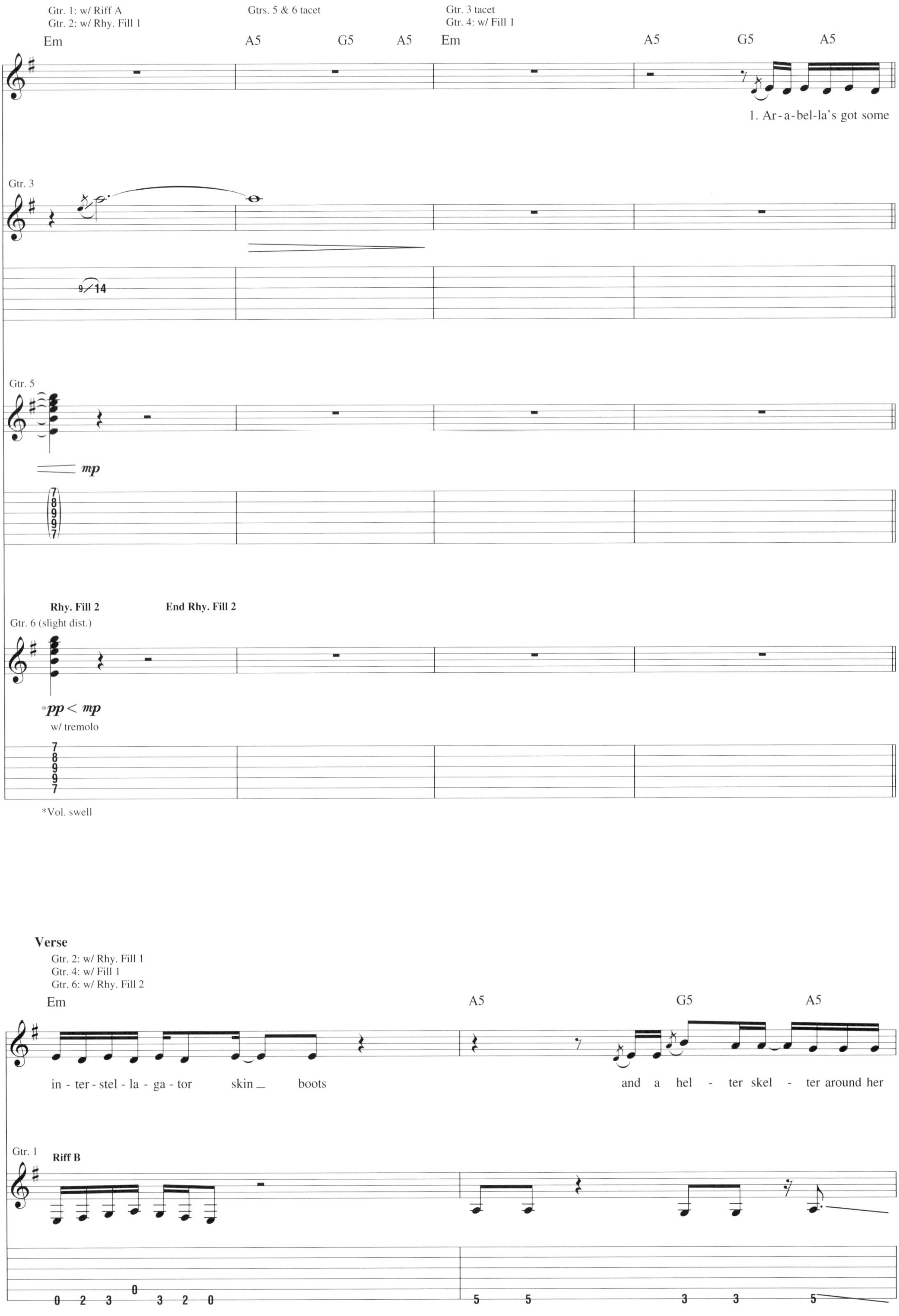
Gtr. 1: w/ Riff A
Gtr. 2: w/ Rhy. Fill 1
Gtrs. 5 & 6 tacet
Gtr. 3 tacet
Gtr. 4: w/ Fill 1
Em
A5
G5
A5
Em
A5
G5
A5
1. Ar - a - bel - la's got some
Gtr. 3
Gtr. 5
mp
Rhy. Fill 2
End Rhy. Fill 2
Gtr. 6 (slight dist.)
*pp < mp
w/ tremolo
*Vol. swell
Verse
Gtr. 2: w/ Rhy. Fill 1
Gtr. 4: w/ Fill 1
Gtr. 6: w/ Rhy. Fill 2
Em
A5
G5
A5
in - ter - stel - la - ga - tor skin_ boots
and a hel - ter skel - ter around her
Gtr. 1
Riff B

Chorus

As Ar-a-bel-la,

Rhy. Fig. 1 — **End Rhy. Fig. 1**

1st time, Gtrs. 7 & 8: w/ Rhy. Fig. 1 (3 times)
2nd time, Gtrs. 7 & 8: w/ Rhy. Fig. 1 (2 1/2 times)

As Ar-a-bel-la. Just might have tapped in-to your

To Coda

mind and soul. You can't be sure.

Interlude

Gtr. 1: w/ Riff A
Gtr. 6 tacet
Gtr. 2 tacet
Gtr. 4: w/ Fill 1

2. Ar-a-

Gtr. 2 — **Rhy. Fill 3** — **End Rhy. Fill 3**

Gtr. 6 — **Rhy. Fill 3A** — **End Rhy. Fill 3A**

Verse

bel-la's got a '70s head, she's a mod-ern lov-er. It's an ex-plo-ra-tion; she's made of out-er space. And her lips are like the gal-ax-y's edge, and a kiss the col-our of a con-stel-la-tion fall-ing in-to place.

D.S. al Coda

⊕ Coda

Bridge

___ be sure. ___ ...in a chee-tah print
That's mag-ic...

*Composite arrangement

A5
E5
coat. Just a slip... ...un - der - neath it I hope. Ask - ing if... ...I can have one of
let ring
G5
C5
those... ...or - gan - ic... ...cig - a - rettes that she smokes. Wraps her lips... ...round the Mex - i - can
A5
C5
coke. Makes you wish... ...that you were the bot - tle. Takes a sip...) ...of your
D5
D♯5
N.C.
soul and it sounds like...

Guitar Solo

Gtrs. 7 & 8 tacet

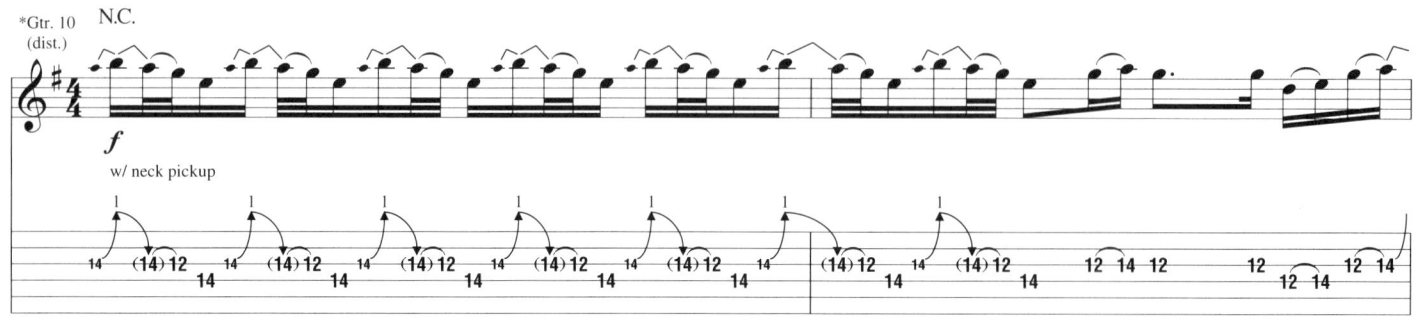

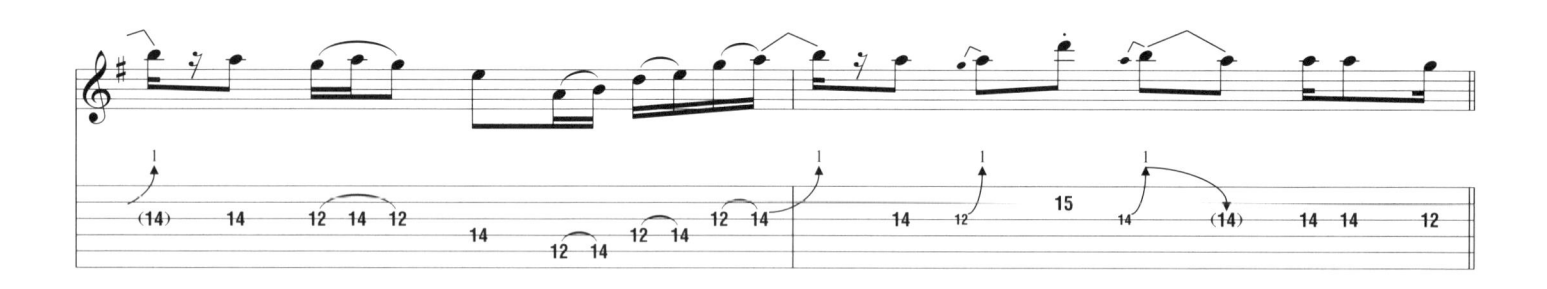

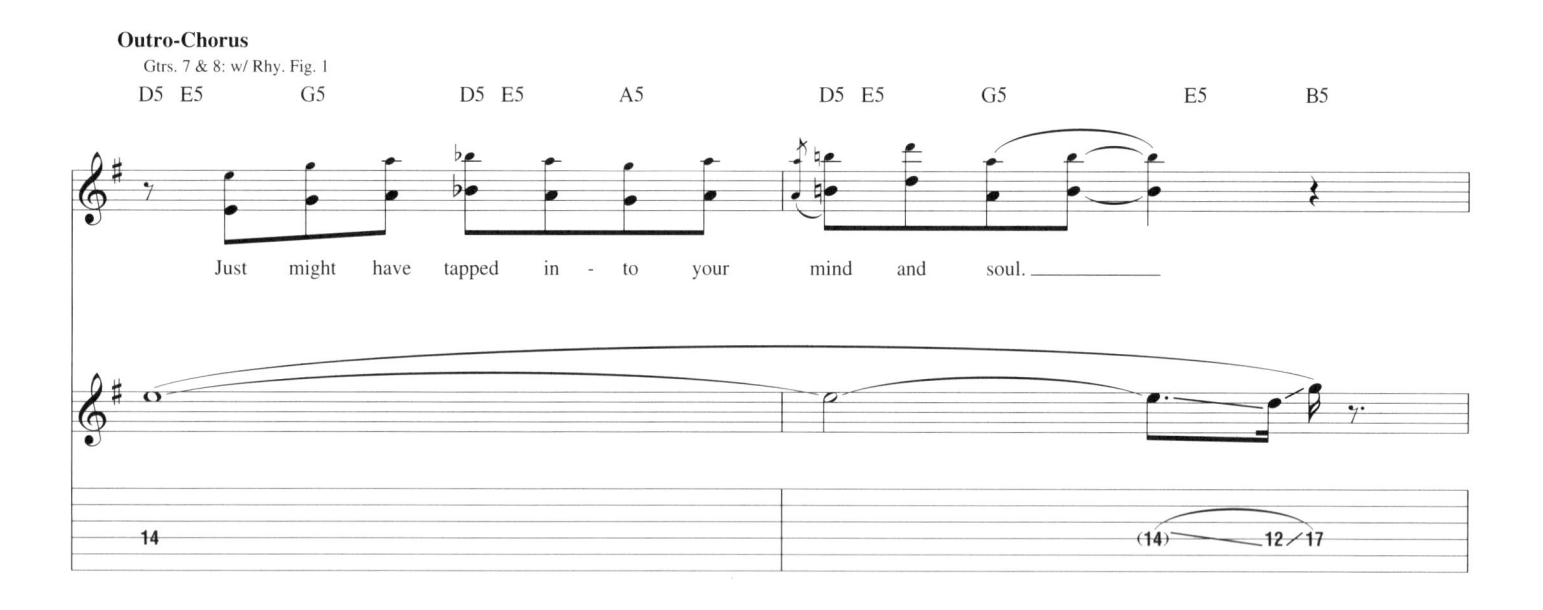

Outro-Chorus

Just might have tapped in - to your mind and soul.

You can't be sure.

I Want It All

Words by Alex Turner
Music by Arctic Monkeys

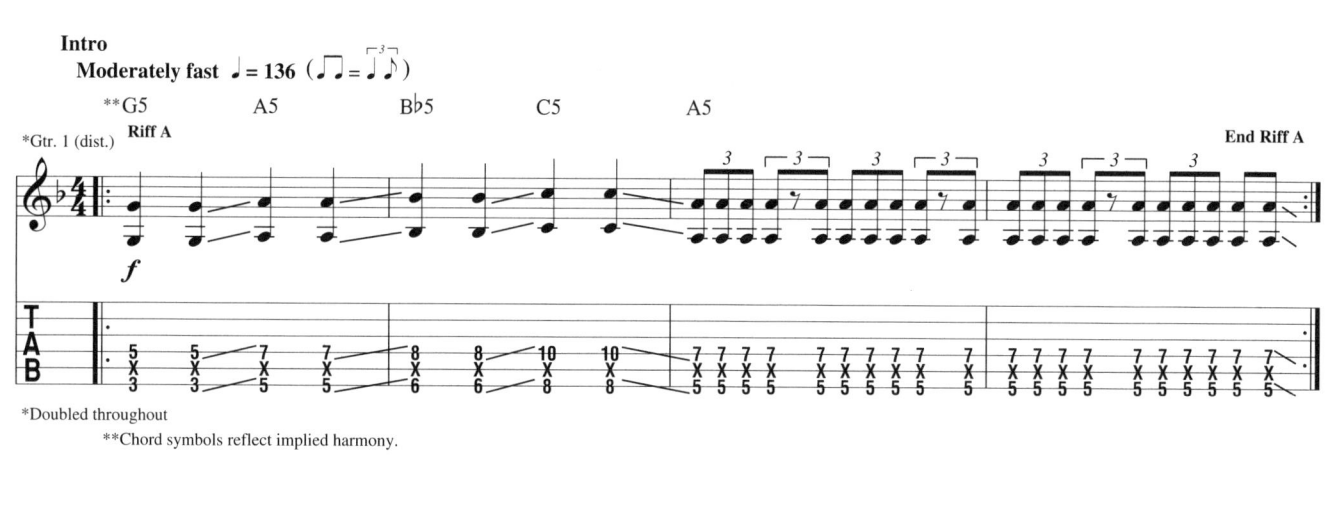

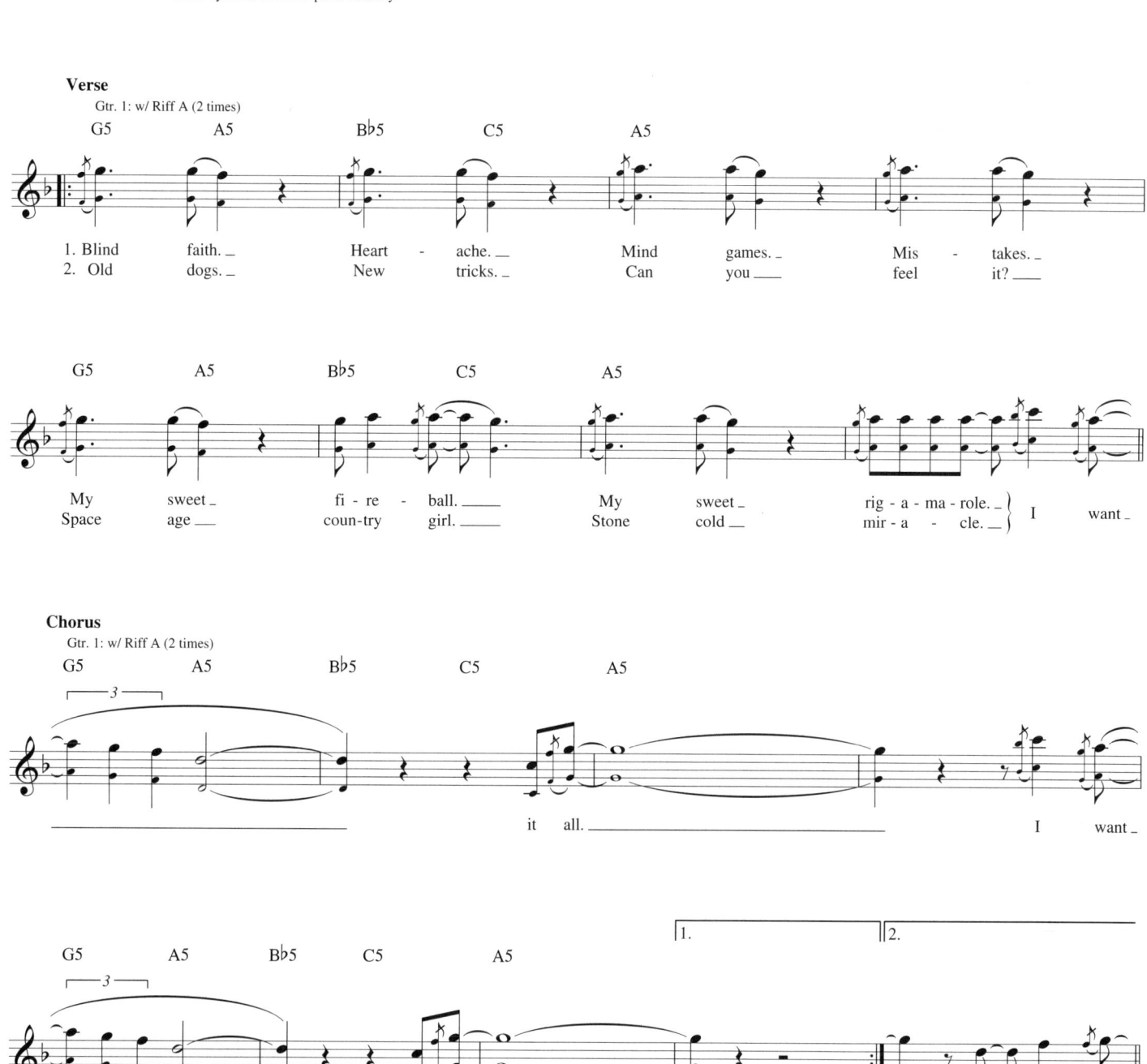

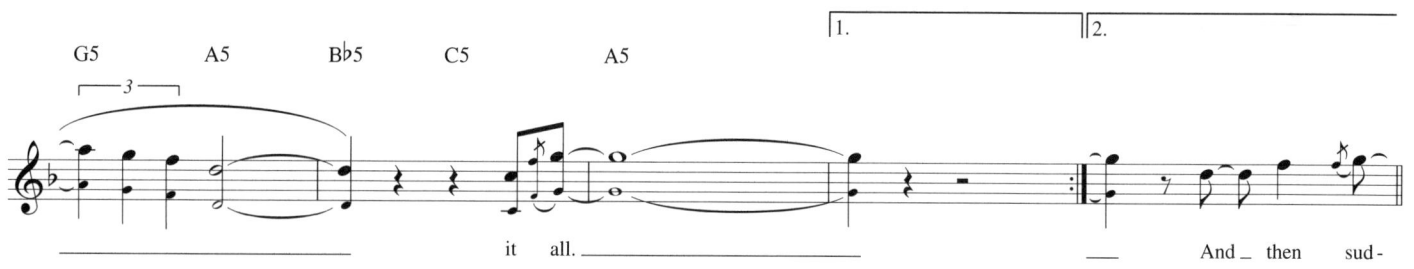

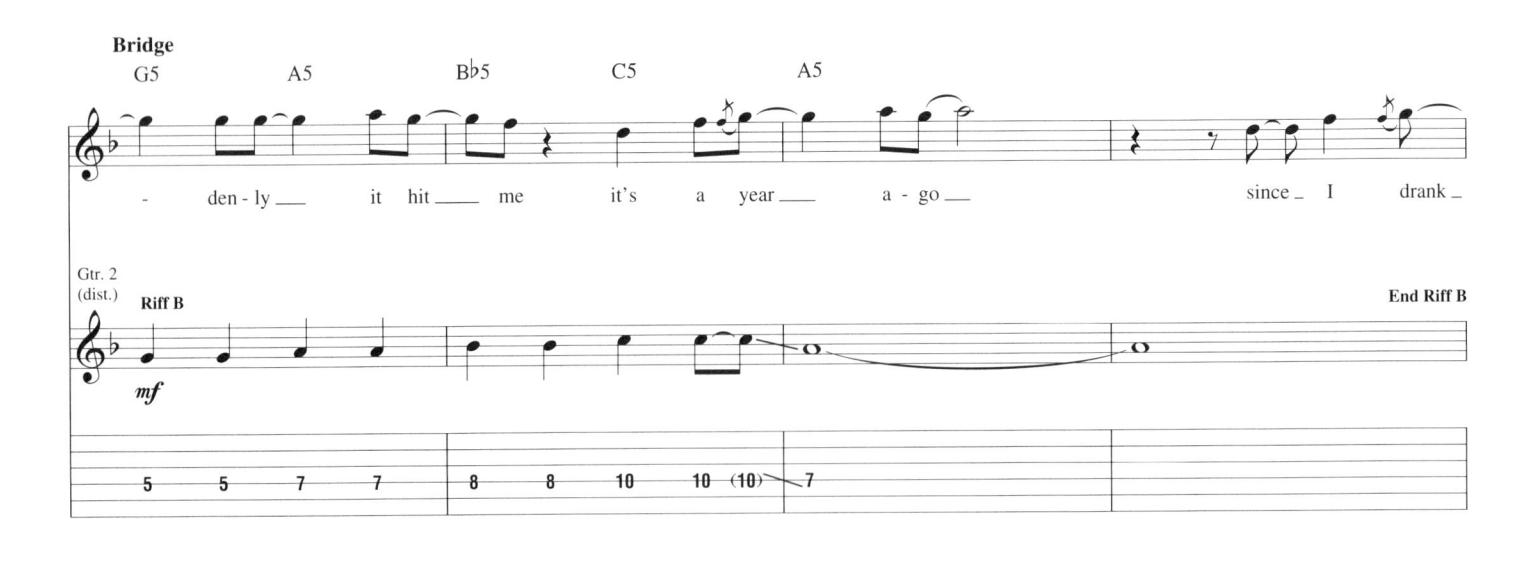

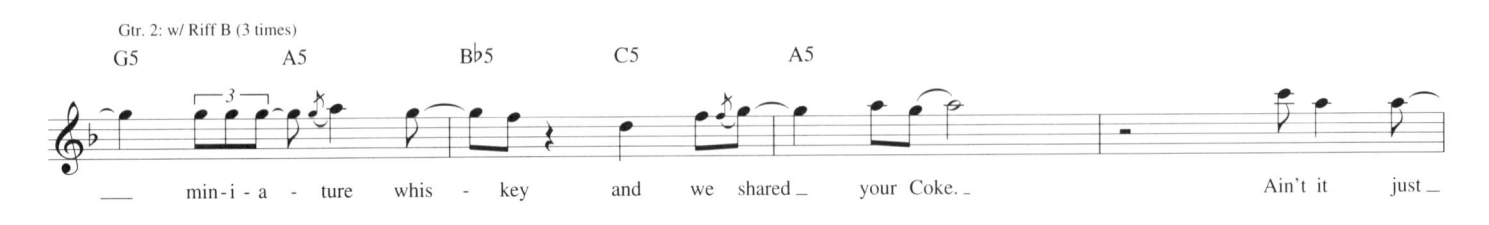

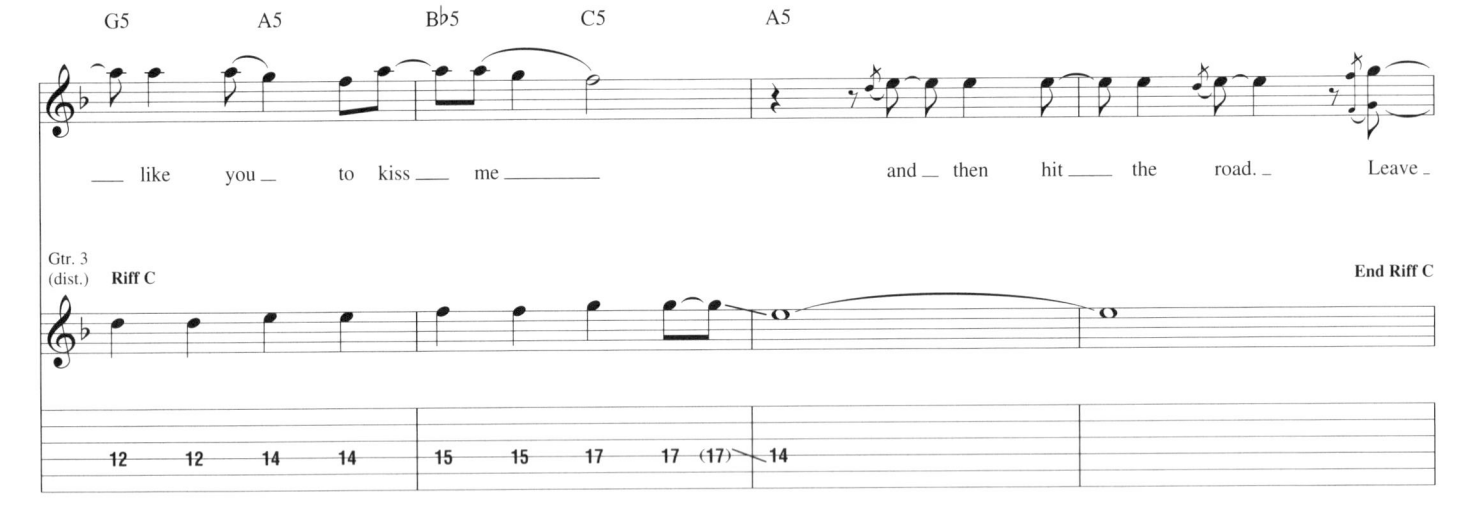

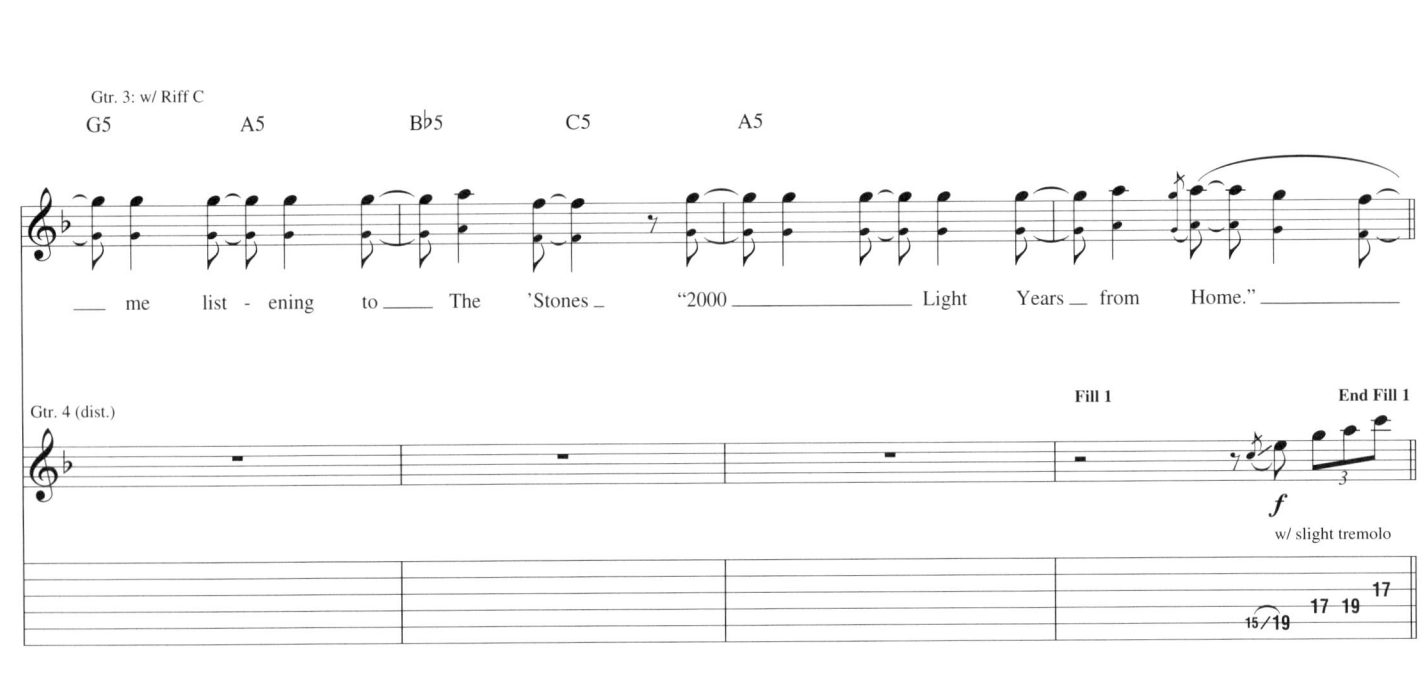

-den-ly it hit me it's a year a-go since I drank mini-a-ture whis-key and we shared your Coke. Ain't it just like you to kiss me and then hit the road. Leave me list-ening to The 'Stones "2000 Light Years from Home."

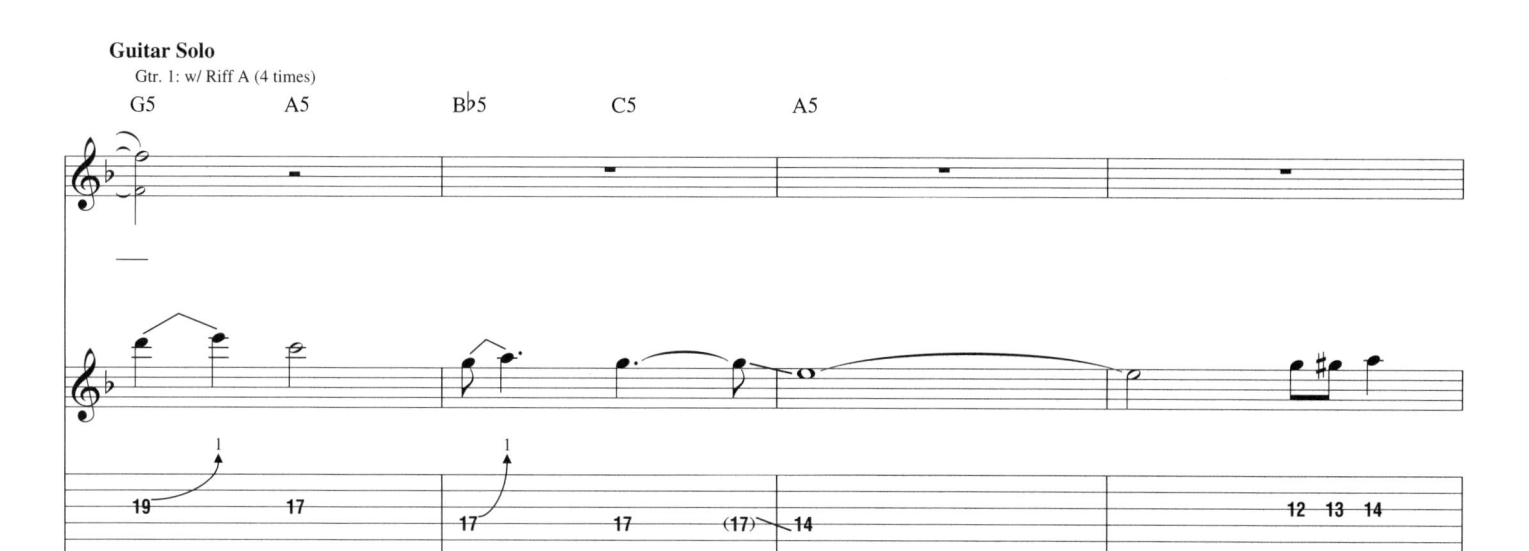

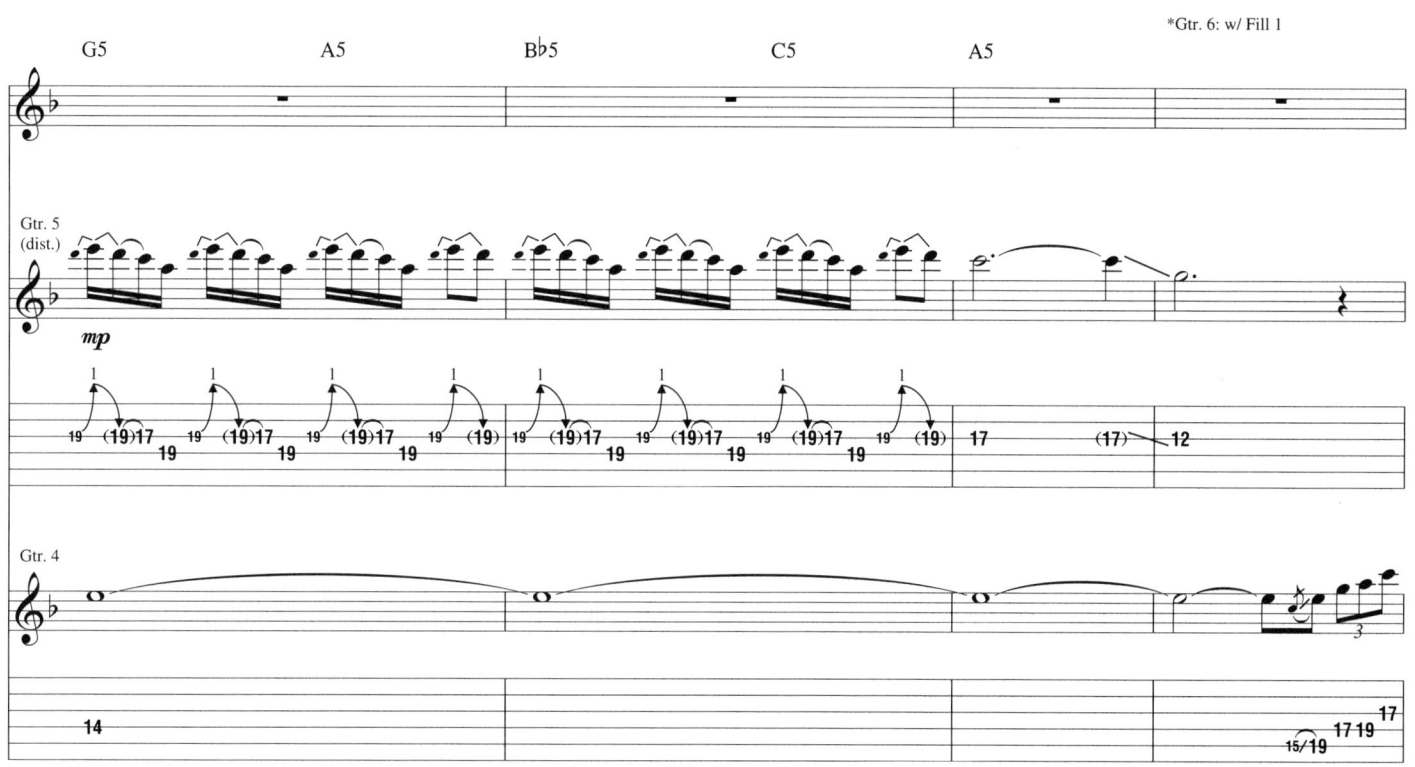

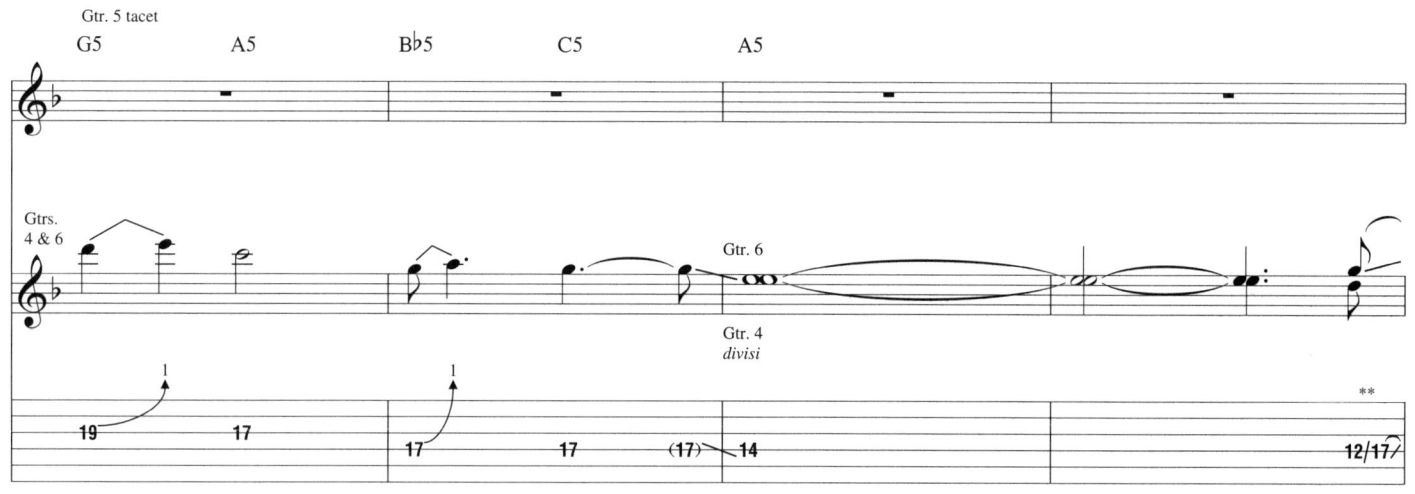

Guitar Solo

44

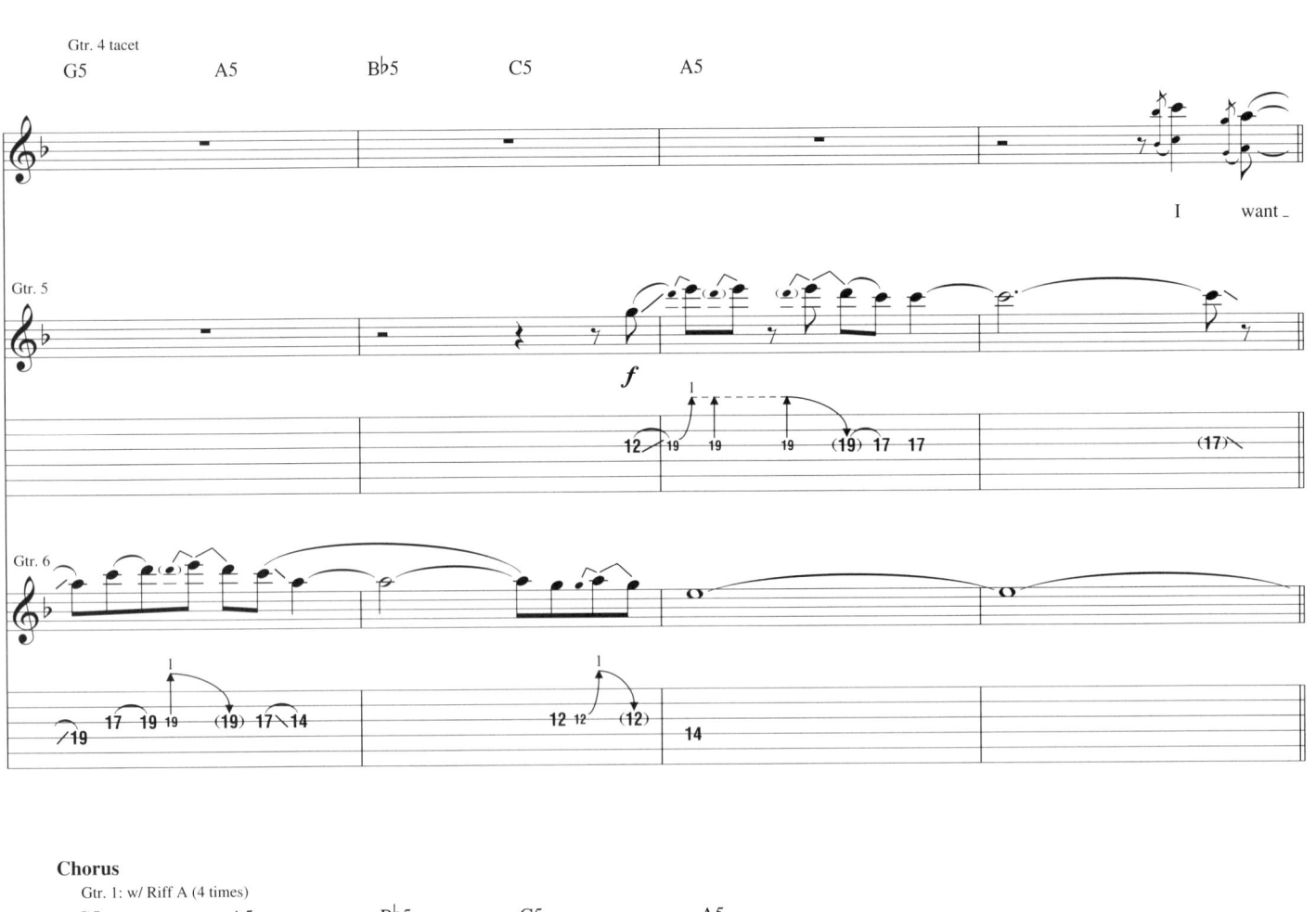

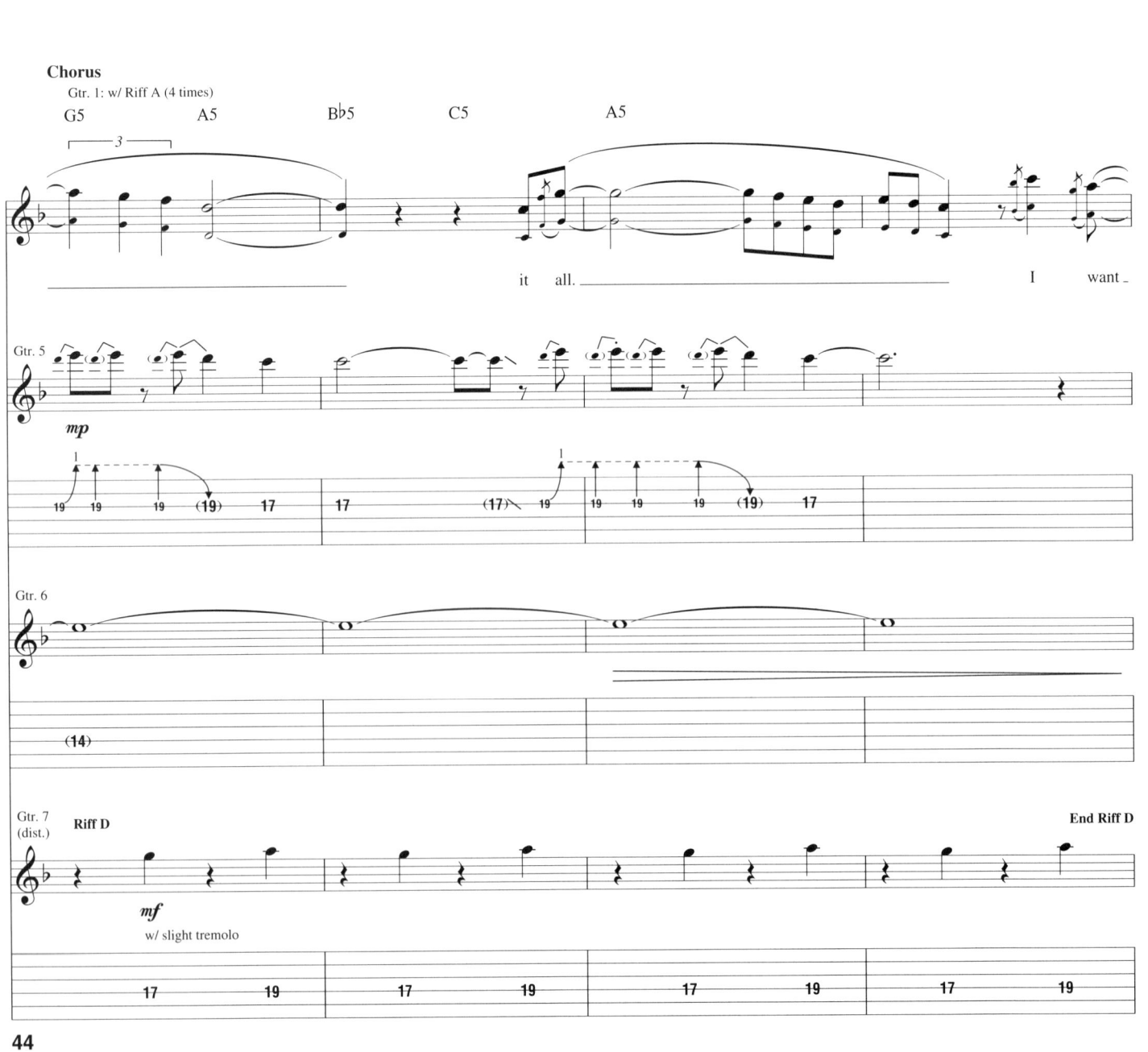

Gtr. 6 tacet
Gtr. 7: w/ Riff D (3 times)
G5 A5 B♭5 C5 A5
it all.
And I want
Gtr. 5
G5 A5 B♭5 C5 A5
it all.
And I want
G5 A5 B♭5 C5 A5
it all.
Outro
Begin fade
Gtr. 1: w/ Riff A (till fade)
Gtr. 7: w/ Riff D (till fade)
G5 A5 B♭5 C5 A5
*Played ahead of the beat.
Gtr. 7 tacet
Fade out
G5 A5 B♭5 C5 A5 G5 A5 B♭5 C5 A5

No. 1 Party Anthem

Words by Alex Turner
Music by Arctic Monkeys

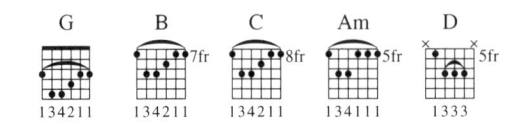

Verse
Slow ♩ = 60

1. So you're on the prowl, wondering whether she left already or not.

Leather jacket collar popped like antenna, never knowing when to stop.

*Piano arr. for gtr.
**See top of page for chord diagrams pertaining to rhythm slashes.
***Vol. swells

© 2013 EMI MUSIC PUBLISHING LTD.
All Rights in the U.S. and Canada Controlled and Administered by EMI APRIL MUSIC INC.
All Rights Reserved   International Copyright Secured   Used by Permission

Verse

Sun-glass-es in-doors, par for the course, lights in the floors and sweat on the walls, cag-es and poles.

2. Call off the search for your soul or put it on hold a-gain. She's hav-ing a sly in-door smoke, she calls the folks who run this her old-est friends. Sip-ping her drink and laugh-

47

Lyrics:
ing at imaginary jokes as all the signals are sent. Her eyes invite you to approach, and it seems as though those lumps in your throat that you just swallowed have got you going—

Chorus
Come on, come on, come on. Come on, come on, come on.

*Chord symbols reflect implied harmony.

| C | Cm | G |

Number one party anthem.

End Riff A1

let ring

End Riff A

let ring

Verse

Gtr. 3: w/ Rhy. Fig. 3
Gtr. 5 tacet

| G | B | C |

3. She's a certified mind-blower, knowing full well that I don't

Gtr. 4

| Am | D | G |

I may suggest there's somewhere from which I might know her just to get the ball to roll.

49

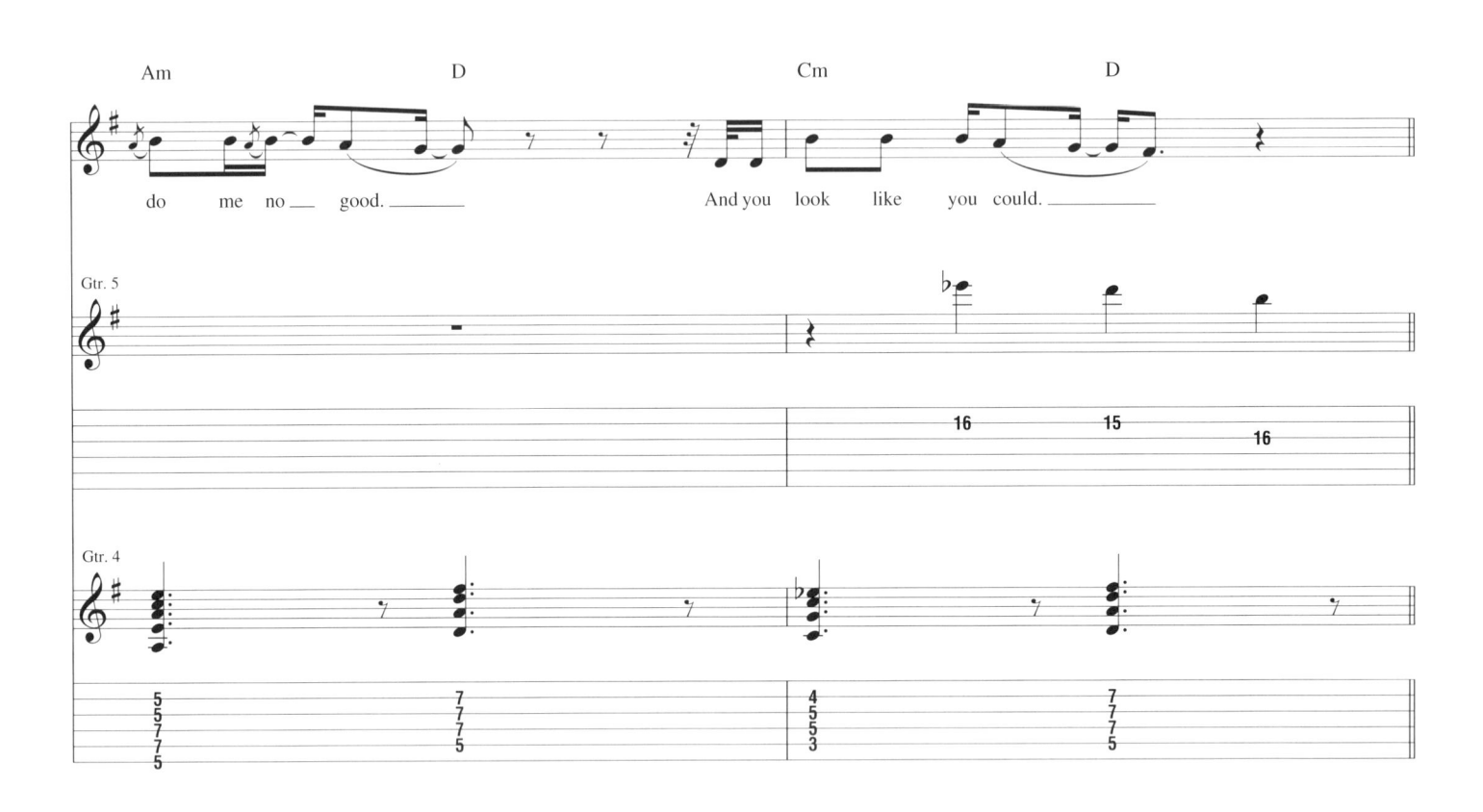

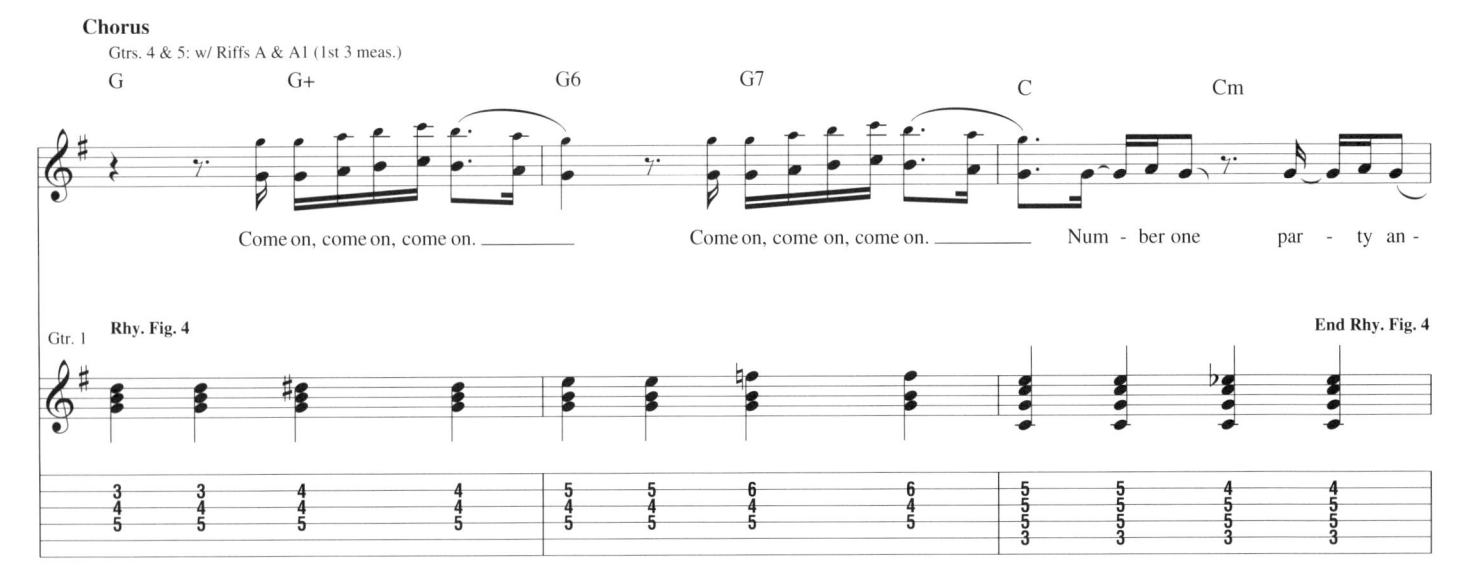

Drunk-en mon-o-logues, con-fused be-cause it's not like I'm fall-ing in love; I just want you to do me no good. And you look like you could.

Chorus
Gtrs. 4 & 5: w/ Riffs A & A1 (1st 3 meas.)

Come on, come on, come on. Come on, come on, come on. Num-ber one par-ty an-

50

Gtr. 1: w/ Rhy. Fig. 4
Gtrs. 4 & 5: w/ Riffs A & A1
G
G+
G6
G7
- them. Come on, come on, come on.
Be - fore the mo - ment's gone.
Gtr. 3
C
Cm
Gtr. 1 tacet
G
G7
Num - ber one par - ty an - them.
*Gtrs. 7 & 8 (elec.)
mp
w/ clean tone & Leslie
mf
*Composite arrangement
Gtr. 6 (elec.)
mf
w/ clean tone & Leslie
Gtr. 3

Bridge

Lyrics:
The look of love. The rush of blood. The "she's with me." The Gallic shrug.
The shutter-bugs. The camera plus. The black and white and the colour dodge. The good-time girls. The cubicles.

Em7
Am
C
D
The house of fun. The num - ber one par - ty an - them.
*Gtr. 9 (elec.)
mp
w/ dist. & Leslie
w/ slide
*Doubled throughout
Gtrs. 7 & 8
Gtr. 7
Gtr. 8
divisi
Gtr. 6
Gtr. 3
Interlude
Gtrs. 3, 6, 7 & 8 tacet
Gtrs. 4 & 5: w/ Riffs A & A1 (1st 3 meas.)
G
G+
G6
G7
C
Cm
Gtr. 9
pp
mf
steady gliss.

Outro

Come on, come on, come on. Come on, come on, come on. Come on, come on, come on.

Come on, come on, come on. Be-fore the mo-ment's gone.

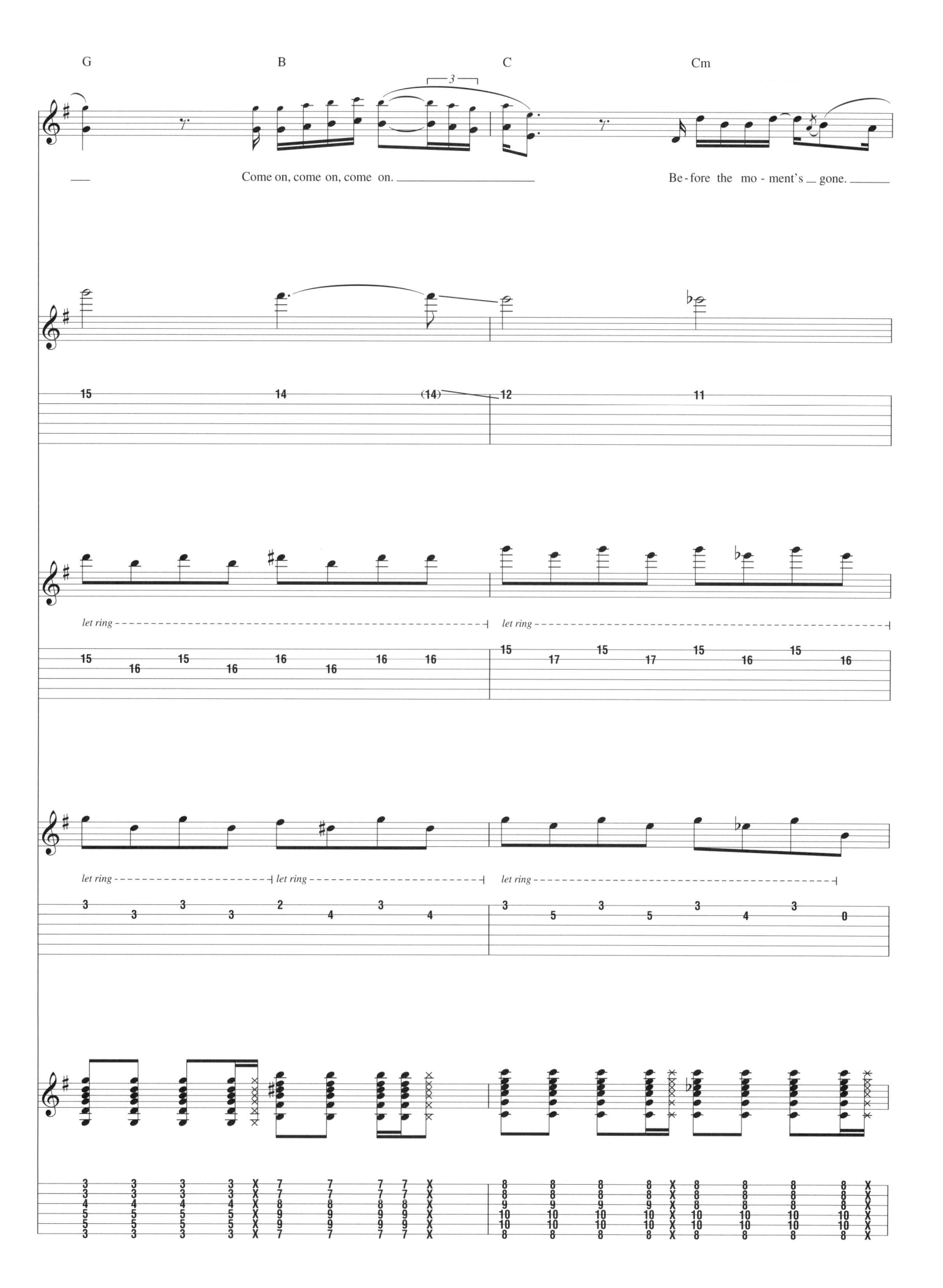

Num - ber one   par - ty an - them. Num - ber one   par - ty an -

-them. Num-ber one   par - ty an - them.

Mad Sounds

Words by Alex Turner and Alan Smyth
Music by Arctic Monkeys

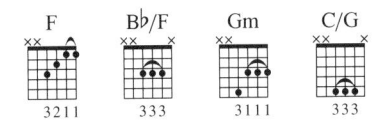

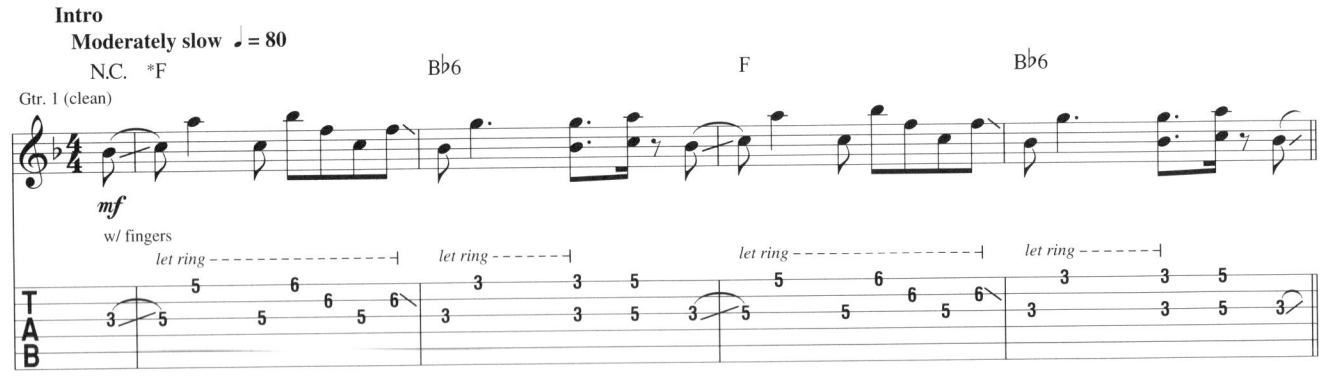

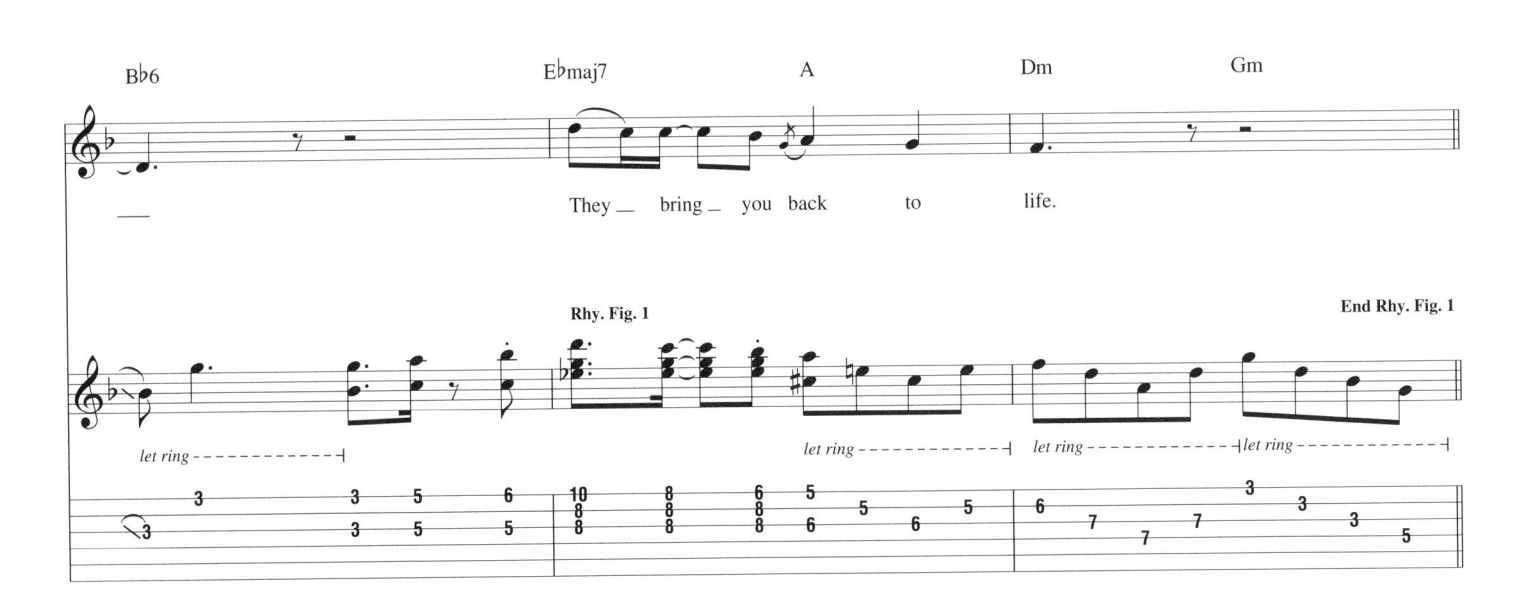

Chorus
Fmaj7
B♭
Mad sounds in your ears.
They make you get up and dance.
Yeah, they make you get up.
Riff A
End Riff A
let ring
F
B♭
Yeah, they make you get up.
Gtr. 1
*Played behind the beat.
Gtr. 2
(clean)
Riff B
End Riff B
mf
w/ Leslie
Verse
Gtr. 2: w/ Riff B
B♭6
2. Love buck-les un - der the strain of those wild nights.

Chorus
Gtr. 1: w/ Rhy. Fig. 1
Gtr. 1: w/ Riff A (2 1/2 times)
E♭maj7 A Dm Gm Fmaj7 B♭ Fmaj7 B♭
Run _ but _ you can - not hide. Mad _ sounds in your ears, _
Rhy. Fig. 2
End Rhy. Fig. 2
Gtr. 2
Gtr. 2: w/ Rhy. Fig. 2 (1 1/2 times)
Fmaj7 B♭ Fmaj7 B♭ Fmaj7 B♭
they make you get up and dance. They make you get up. All _ night long, _
Fmaj7 B♭ Fmaj7 B♭ Fmaj7 B♭ N.C.
they re - ap - pear. _ They make you get up and dance. _ Yeah, they make you get _
Gtr. 1
let ring
(cont. in slashes)
Gtr. 2

Interlude

*F   B♭/F   F   B♭/F

— up. — Sup-

*See top of first page of song for chord diagrams pertaining to rhythm slashes.

Bridge

Gtrs. 1 & 2: w/ Rhy. Figs. 3 & 3A

F   B♭   F   B♭

-pose you've got to do what you got to do. We just weren't feel-ing how we want-ed to. You sit and

Gm   C/G

try some-times but you just can't fig-ure out what went wrong.

Gm   C/G

Then out of no-where, some-bod-y comes and hits you with an

Gtr. 1: w/ Rhy. Fig. 3 (2 times)
Gtr. 2: w/ Rhy. Fig. 3A

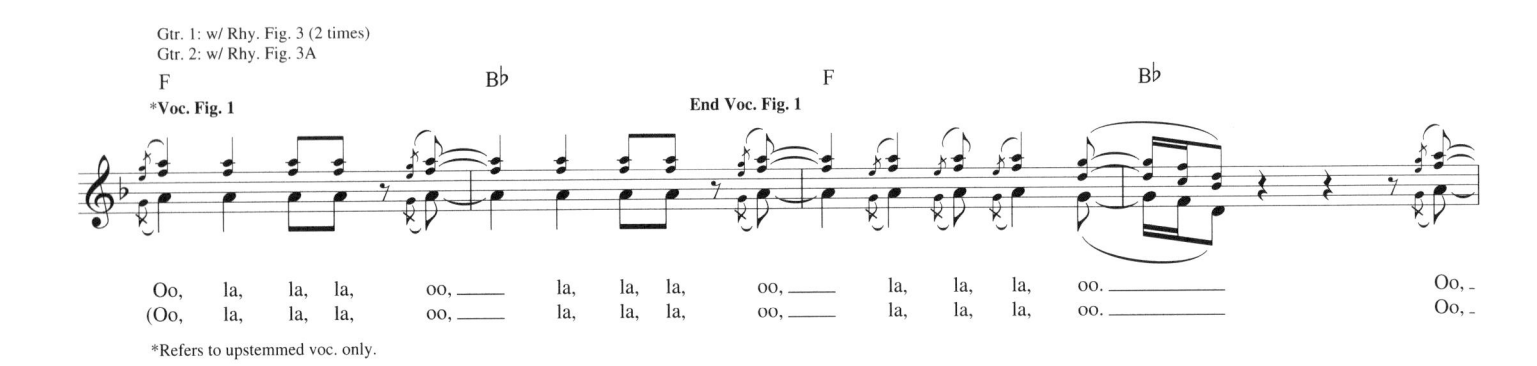

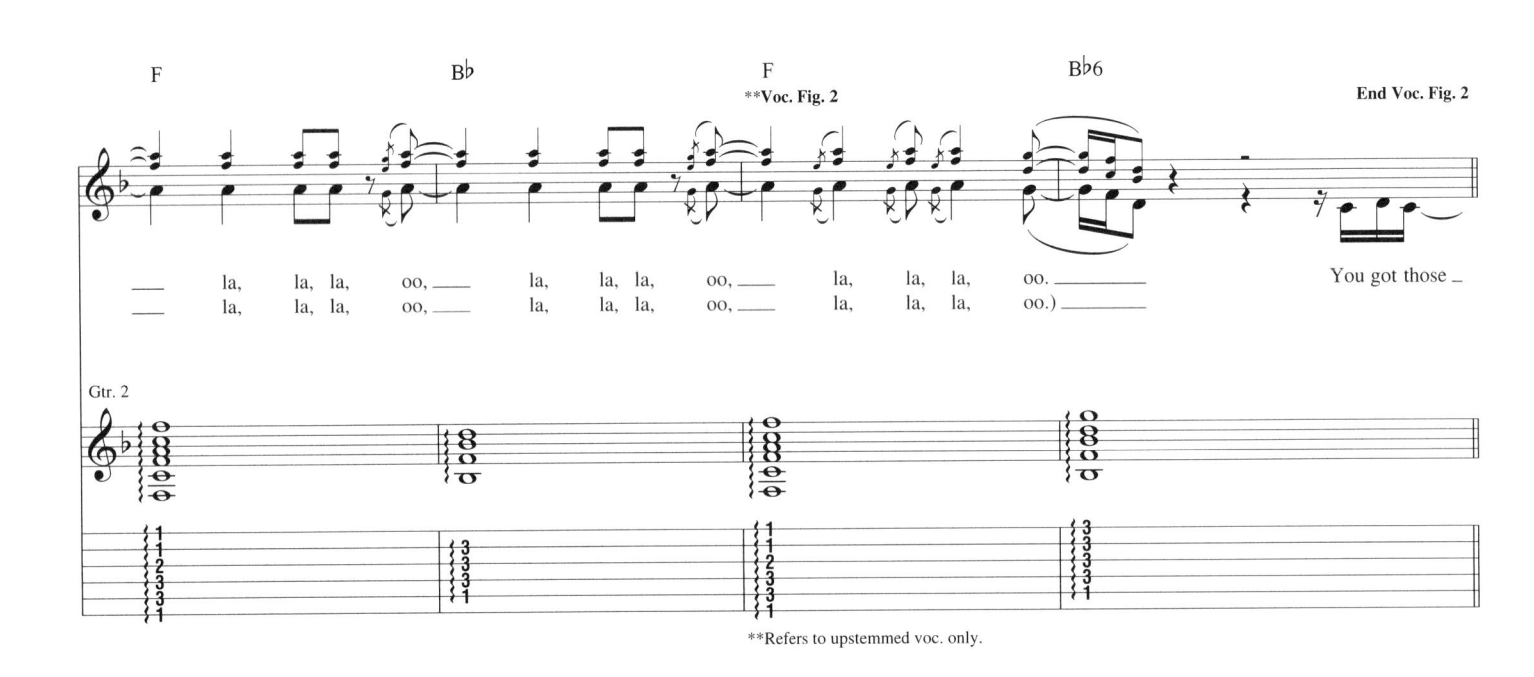

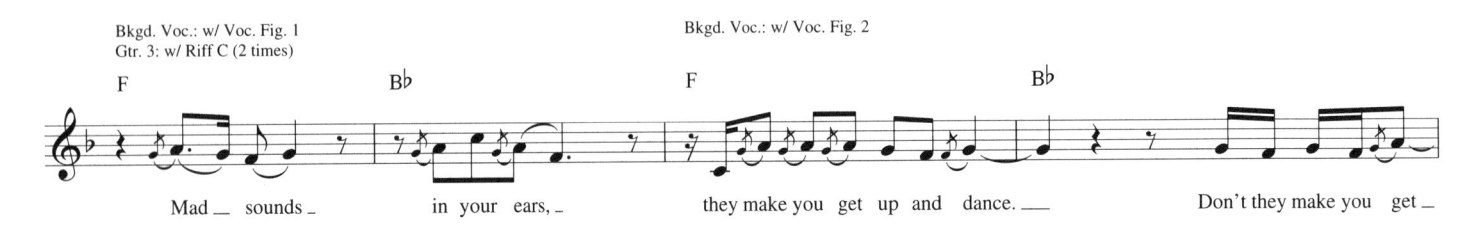

*Voc. Fig. 1 ... End Voc. Fig. 1

Oo, la, la, la, oo, ___ la, la, la, oo, ___ la, la, la, oo. ___ Oo, ___
(Oo, la, la, la, oo, ___ la, la, la, oo, ___ la, la, la, oo. ___ Oo, ___

*Refers to upstemmed voc. only.

**Voc. Fig. 2 ... End Voc. Fig. 2

___ la, la, la, oo, ___ la, la, la, oo, ___ la, la, la, oo. ___ You got those ___
___ la, la, la, oo, ___ la, la, la, oo, ___ la, la, la, oo.) ___

Gtr. 2

**Refers to upstemmed voc. only.

Outro

Bkgd. Voc.: w/ Voc. Fig. 1
Gtrs. 1 & 2: w/ Rhy. Figs. 3 & 3A (3 times)

Bkgd. Voc.: w/ Voc. Fig. 2

___ mad sounds in your ears ___ to make you get up and dance. ___

Gtr. 3 (clean) Riff C ... End Riff C

mf

Bkgd. Voc.: w/ Voc. Fig. 1
Gtr. 3: w/ Riff C (2 times)

Bkgd. Voc.: w/ Voc. Fig. 2

Mad ___ sounds ___ in your ears, ___ they make you get up and dance. ___ Don't they make you get

Bkgd. Voc.: w/ Voc. Fig. 1
F
B♭
Bkgd. Voc.: w/ Voc. Fig. 2
F
B♭
up?
Yeah, they make you get up.
Gtr. 4 (clean)
mf
Bkgd. Voc.: w/ Voc. Fig. 1
F
B♭
Bkgd. Voc.: w/ Voc. Fig. 2
F
B♭
F
Gtr. 4
Gtr. 1
Gtr. 2
Gtr. 3

Fireside

Words by Alex Turner
Music by Arctic Monkeys

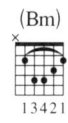

(Bm)

Gtrs. 1, 2, 4 & 6: Capo III

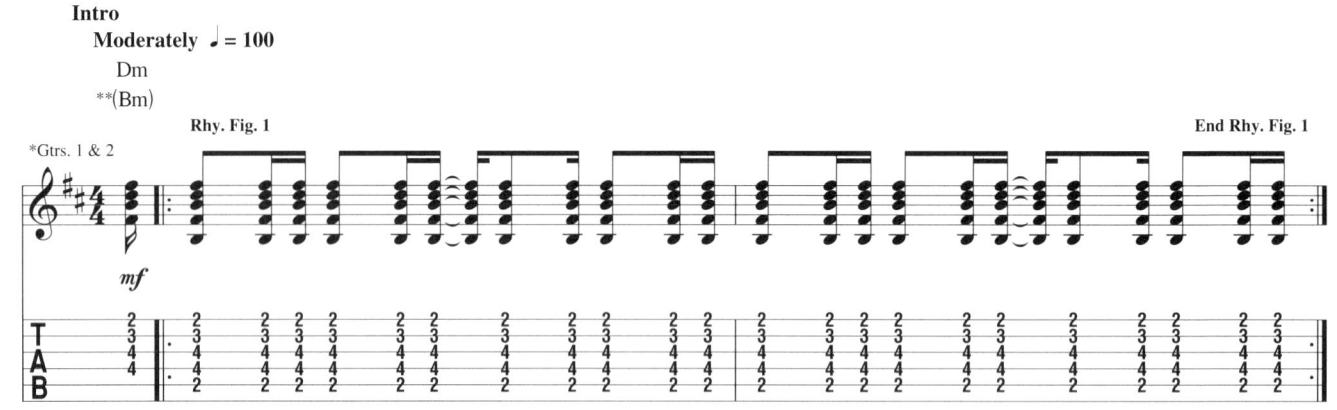

Intro
Moderately ♩ = 100
Dm
**(Bm)

*Gtr. 1 (acous.); Gtr. 2 (elec.) w/ clean tone; composite arrangement.
**Symbols in parentheses represent chord names respective to capoed guitars.
Symbols above represent actual sounding chords. Capoed fret is "0" in tab.

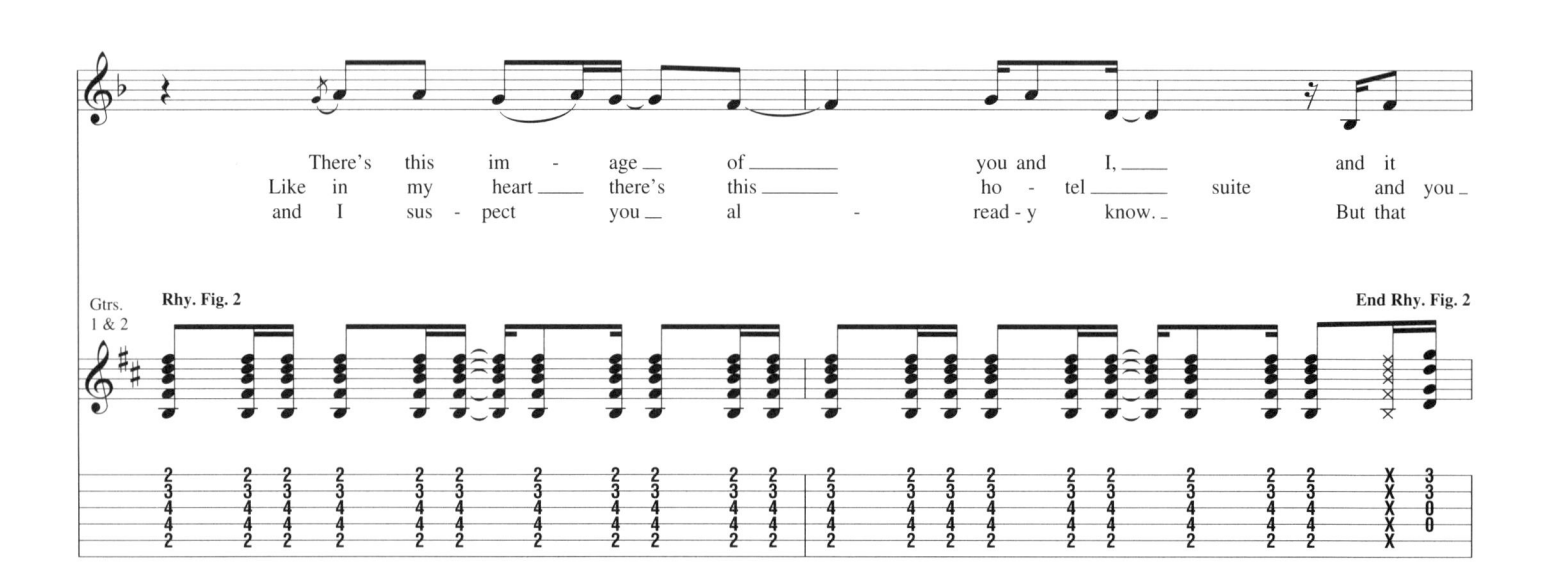

Verse
Gtrs. 1 & 2: w/ Rhy. Fig. 1
Dm
(Bm)

1. I can't explain___ but I___ want to try.___
2. There's all these secrets___ that___ I can't___ keep.
3. There's all those places___ we___ used to go,___

There's this image___ of___ you and I,___ and it
Like in my heart___ there's this___ hotel___ suite___ and you
and I suspect you al- ready know.___ But that

© 2013 EMI MUSIC PUBLISHING LTD.
All Rights in the U.S. and Canada Controlled and Administered by EMI APRIL MUSIC INC.
All Rights Reserved International Copyright Secured Used by Permission

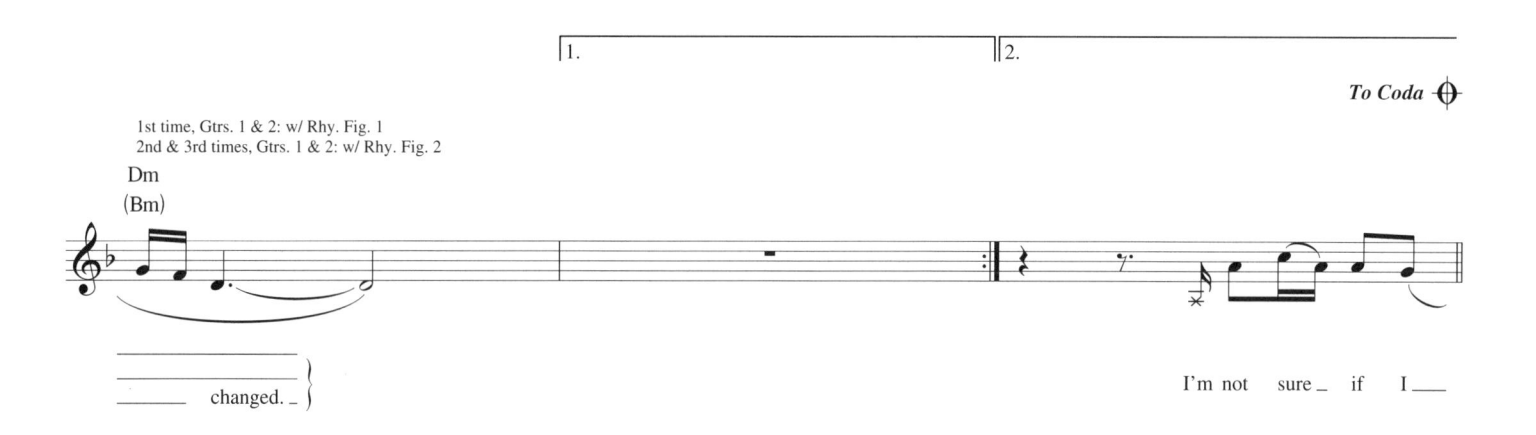

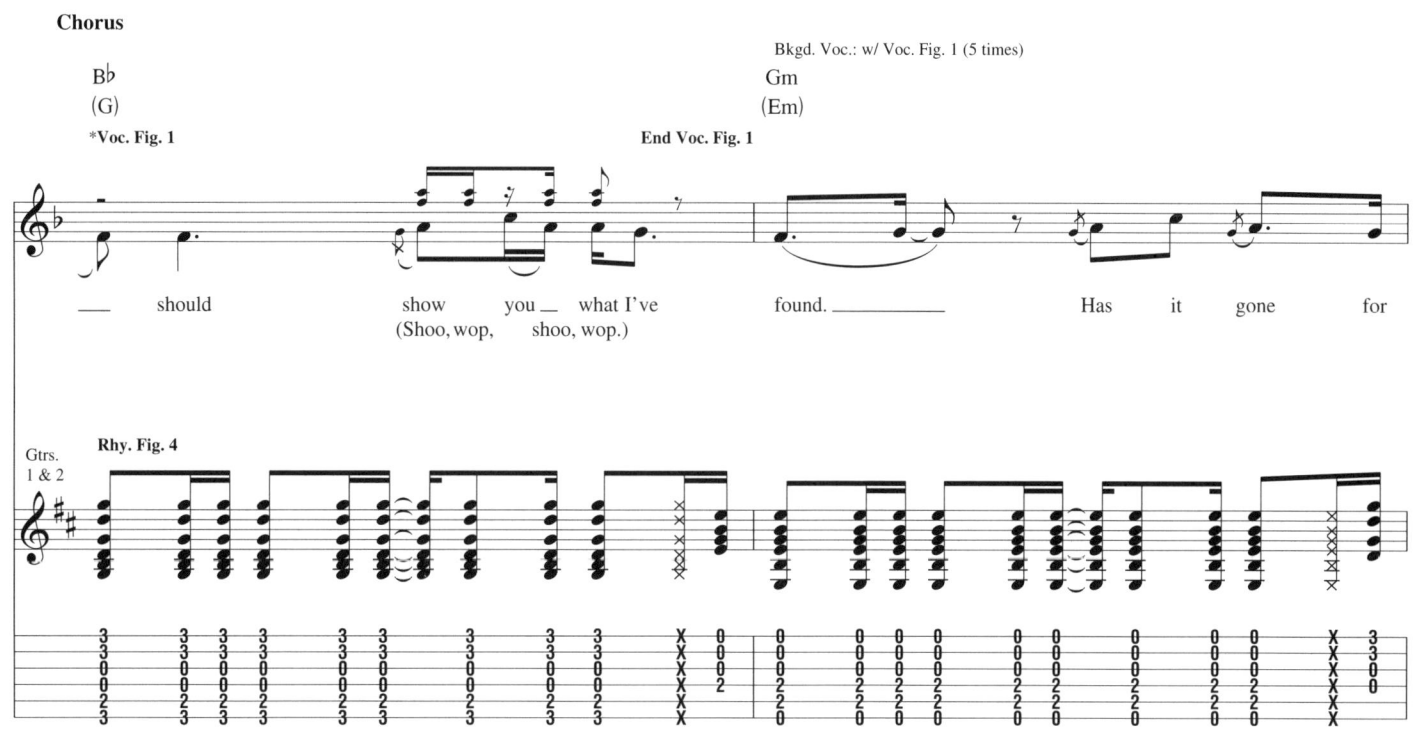

goes _ danc - ing by _ in the morn - ing _ and in the night - time. _
_ lived there _ so long, it's kind - a strange _ now you're gone. _
place on _ mem - o - ry lane you liked _ still looks the same but some - thing a - bout _ it's

1st time, Gtrs. 1 & 2: w/ Rhy. Fig. 1
2nd & 3rd times, Gtrs. 1 & 2: w/ Rhy. Fig. 2

|1. changed. _ | |2. I'm not sure _ if I _

Chorus

_ should show you _ what I've found. _ Has it gone for
(Shoo, wop, shoo, wop.)

*Refers to upstemmed voc. only.

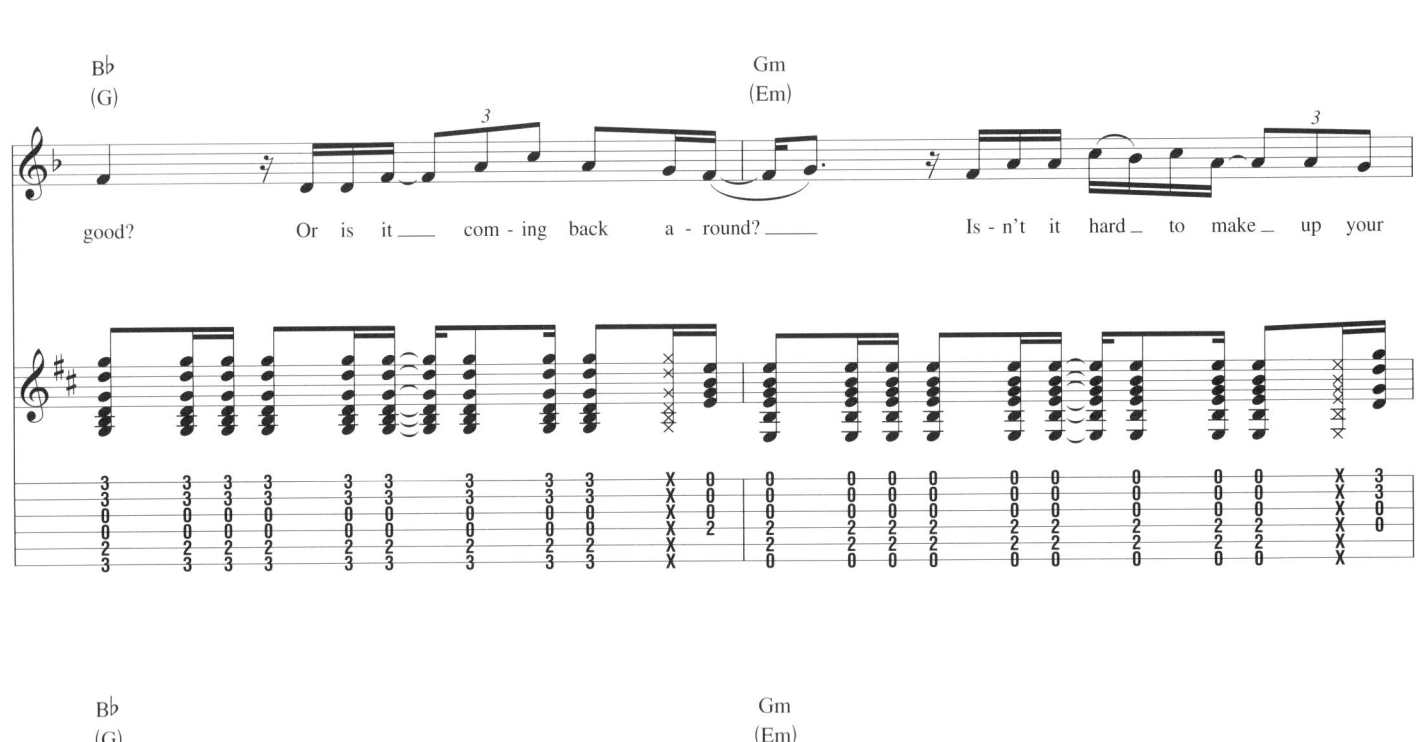

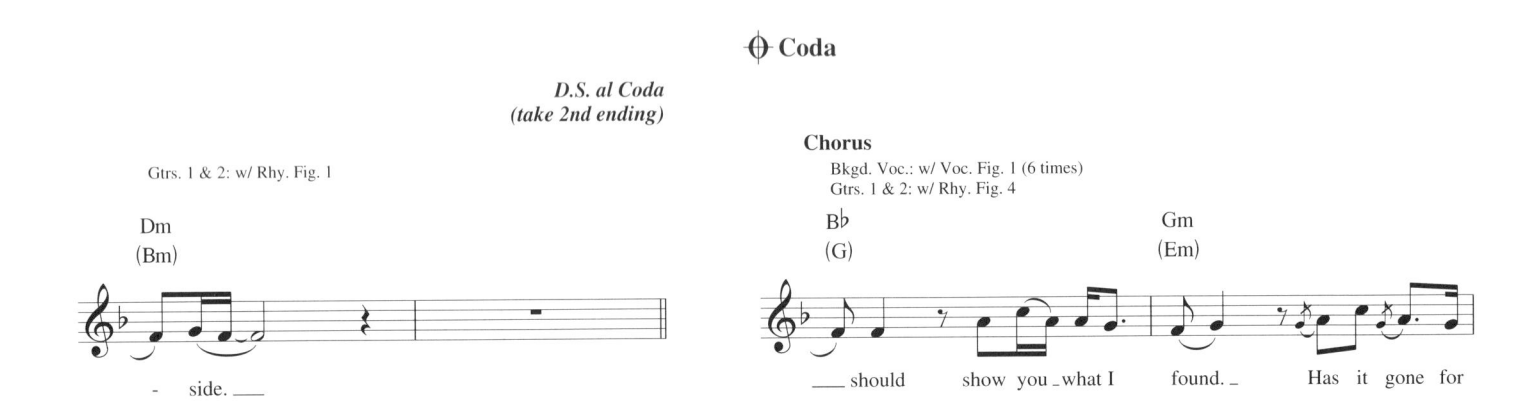

Lyrics

good? Or is it coming back around? Isn't it hard to make up your mind? When you're losing and your fuse is fire-

End Rhy. Fig. 4

Coda

D.S. al Coda
(take 2nd ending)

Gtrs. 1 & 2: w/ Rhy. Fig. 1

Dm (Bm)
-side.

Chorus
Bkgd. Voc.: w/ Voc. Fig. 1 (6 times)
Gtrs. 1 & 2: w/ Rhy. Fig. 4

Bb (G) Gm (Em)
should show you what I found. Has it gone for

Bb (G) Gm (Em) Bb (G)
good? Or is it coming back around? Isn't it hard to make up your mind? When you're

Gtrs. 1 & 2: w/ Rhy. Fig. 2
Gm
(Em)
Dm
(Bm)
los - ing and your fuse is fire - side.
And I thought I
Gtrs. 1 & 2: w/ Rhy. Fig. 4
Bkgd. Voc.: w/ Voc. Fig. 2 (5 times)
B♭
(G)
Gm
(Em)
*Voc. Fig. 2
End Voc. Fig. 2
was yours for - ev - er.
(Shoo, wop, shoo, wop.)
Gtr. 3
(elec.)
mf
w/ dist.
let ring
*Refers to upstemmed voc. only.
B♭
(G)
Gm
(Em)
May - be I was mis - tak - en, but I just can - not man - age
let ring
B♭
(G)
Gm
(Em)
to make it through the day with - out think - ing of you late - ly.
let ring

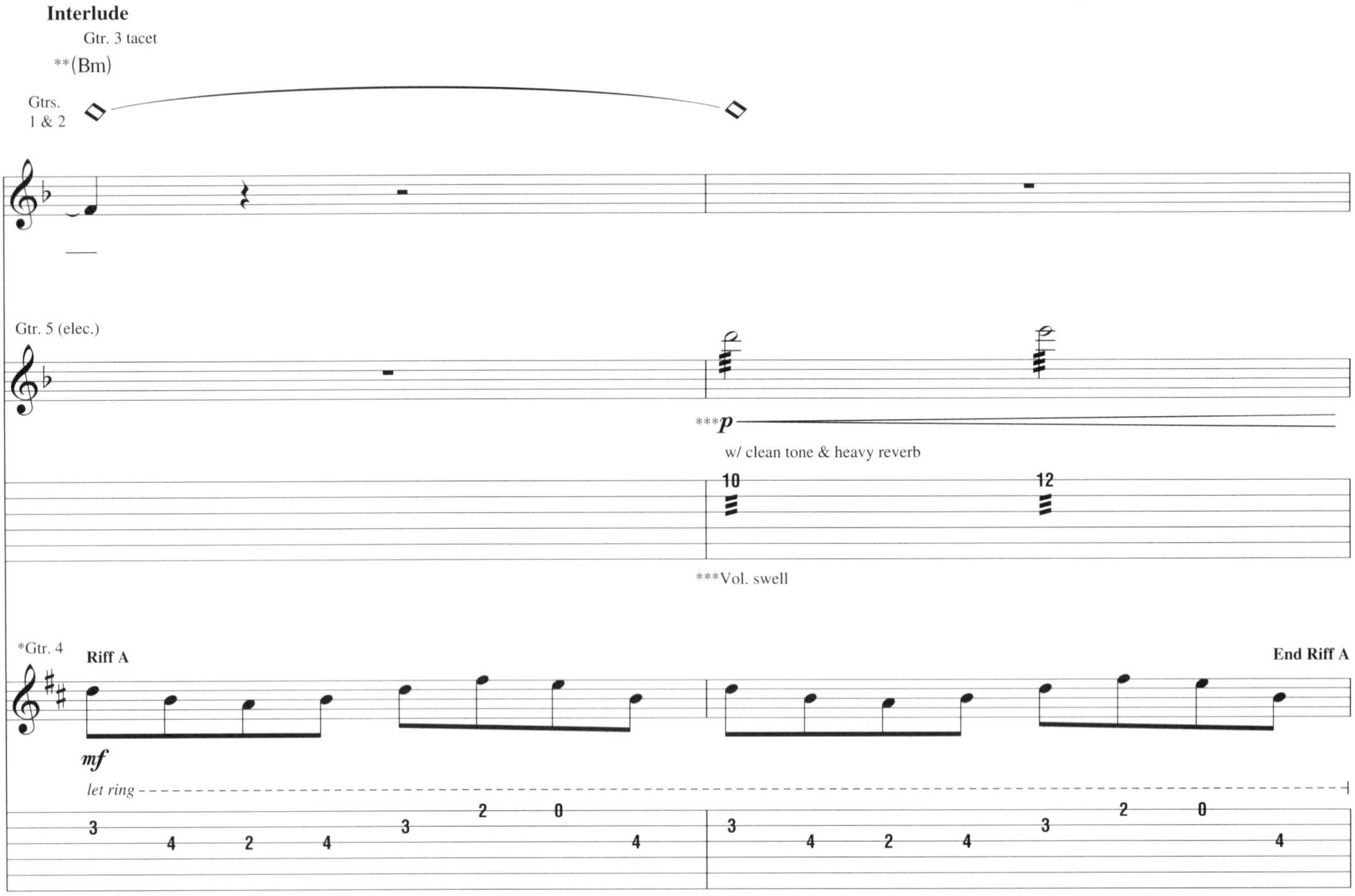

*Clavinet arr. for gtr.

**See top of first page of song for chord diagrams pertaining to rhythm slashes.

Chorus
Bkgd. Voc.: w/ Voc. Fig. 1 (8 times)
Gtrs. 1 & 2: w/ Rhy. Fig. 4 (1st 2 meas.)
Gtr. 4: w/ Riff A (4 times)
B♭ (G)
Gm (Em)
should show you what I found. Has it gone for
Gtr. 5
Gtr. 6 (elec.)
Riff B
End Riff B
mp
w/ clean tone
Gtrs. 1 & 2: w/ Rhy. Fig. 4
Gtr. 5 tacet
Gtr. 6: w/ Riff B (3 times)
B♭ (G)
Gm (Em)
B♭ (G)
good? Or is it com-ing back a-round? Is-n't it hard to make up your mind? When you're
Gm (Em)
B♭ (G)
Gm (Em)
los-ing and your fuse is fire - side.
Outro
Gtrs. 1 & 2: w/ Rhy. Fig. 1 (2 times)
Gtr. 6: w/ Riff B (2 times)
Bkgd. Voc.: w/ Voc. Fig. 1
Dm (Bm)
(Bm)
Gtrs. 1 & 2
Gtr. 4
Gtr. 4
let ring
Gtr. 6
divisi

Why'd You Only Call Me When You're High?

Words by Alex Turner
Music by Arctic Monkeys

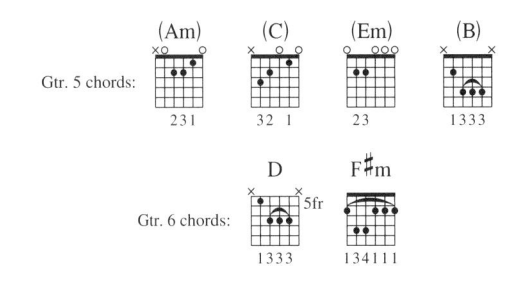

Gtr. 5 chords: (Am) (C) (Em) (B)

Gtr. 6 chords: D F#m

Gtr. 5: Capo II

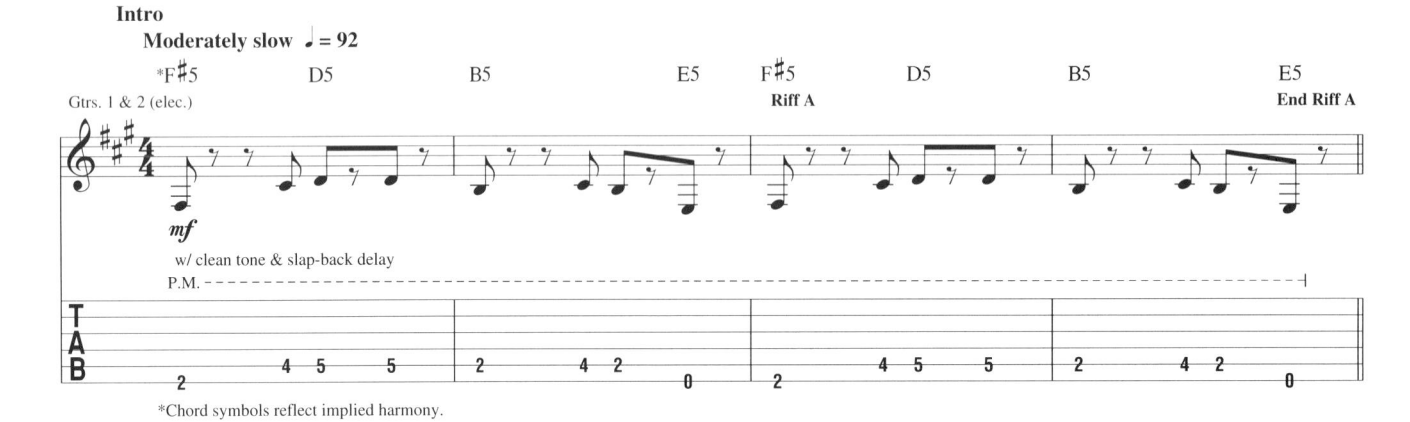

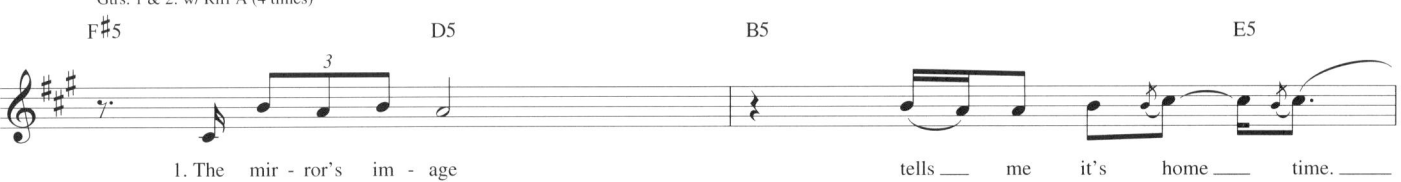

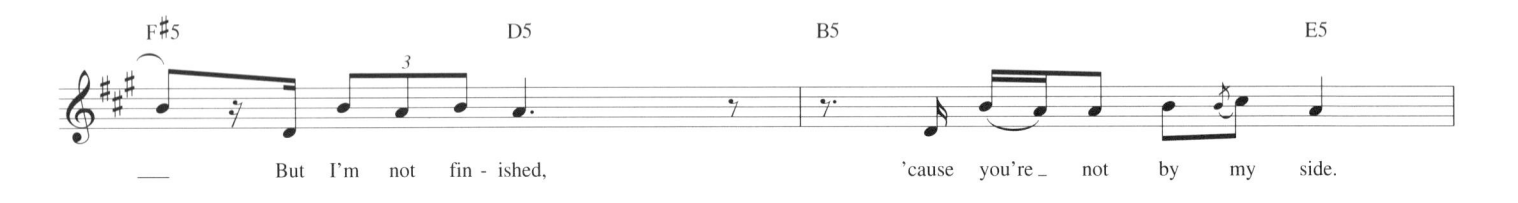

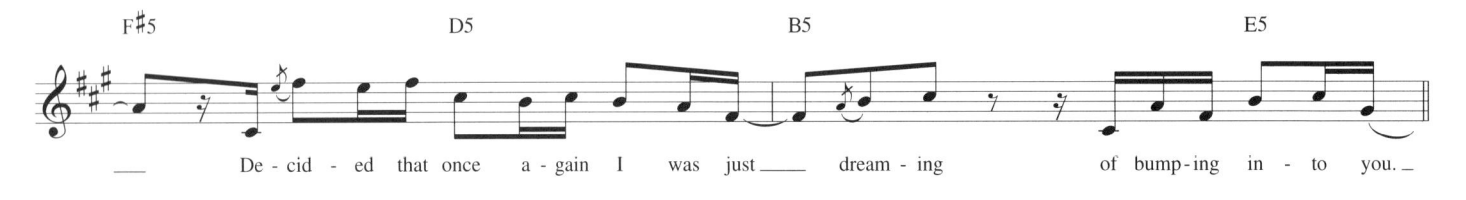

Intro
Moderately slow ♩ = 92

*F#5 D5 B5 E5 F#5 D5 B5 E5

Gtrs. 1 & 2 (elec.)   Riff A   End Riff A

w/ clean tone & slap-back delay
P.M.

*Chord symbols reflect implied harmony.

Verse
Gtrs. 1 & 2: w/ Riff A (4 times)

F#5   D5   B5   E5
1. The mir-ror's im-age   tells __ me it's home __ time. __

F#5   D5   B5   E5
__ But I'm not fin-ished,   'cause you're __ not by my side.

F#5   D5   B5   E5
And as I ar-rived I thought I saw you __ leav-ing car-ry-ing your shoes.

F#5   D5   B5   E5
__ De-cid-ed that once a-gain I was just __ dream-ing of bump-ing in-to you. __

© 2013 EMI MUSIC PUBLISHING LTD.
All Rights in the U.S. and Canada Controlled and Administered by EMI APRIL MUSIC INC.
All Rights Reserved   International Copyright Secured   Used by Permission

Chorus

Now it's three in the morn-ing and I'm try-ing to change your mind. Left you mul-ti-ple missed calls and to my mes-sage you re-plied, "Why'd you on-ly call me when you're high?"

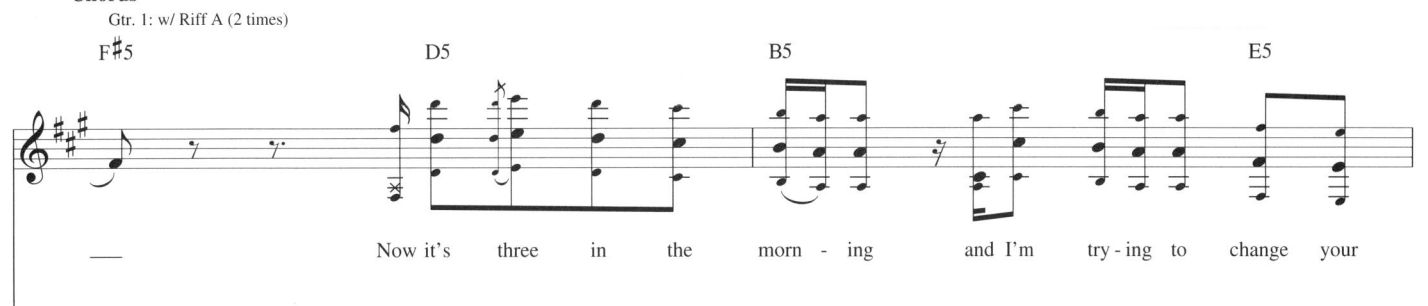

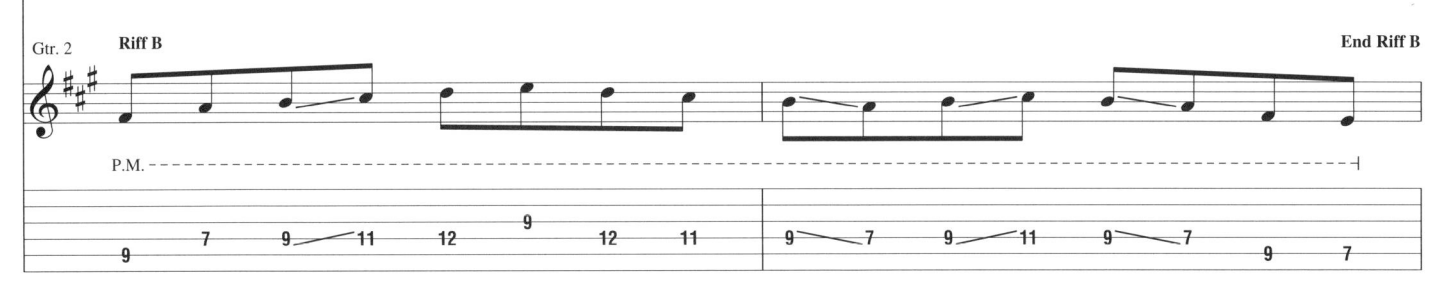

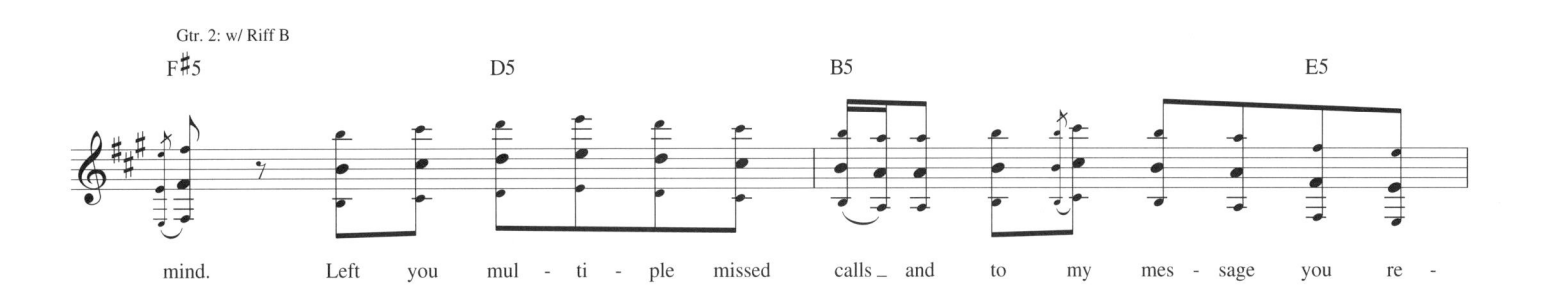

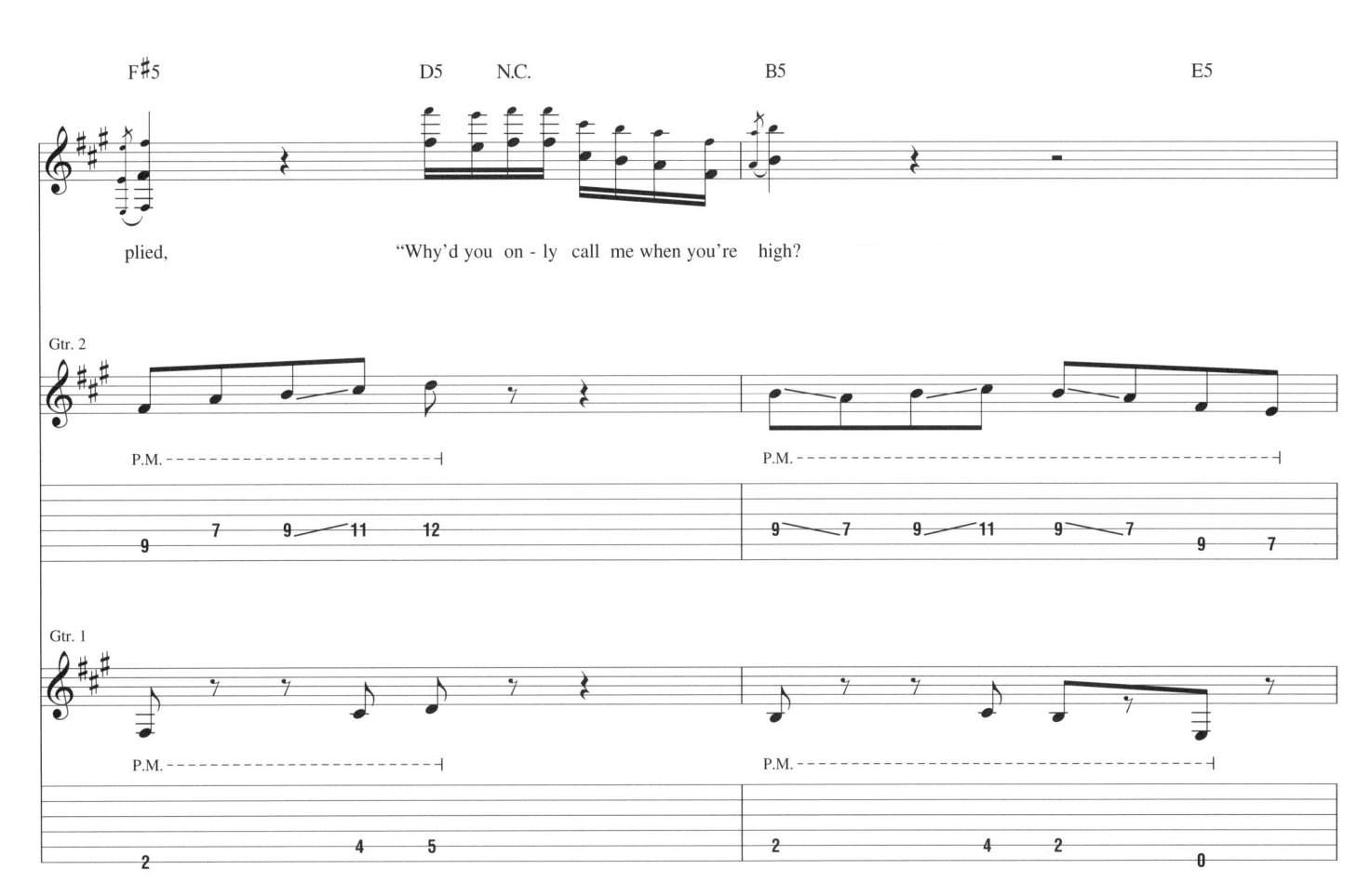

"Hi. Why'd you on-ly call me when you're high?"

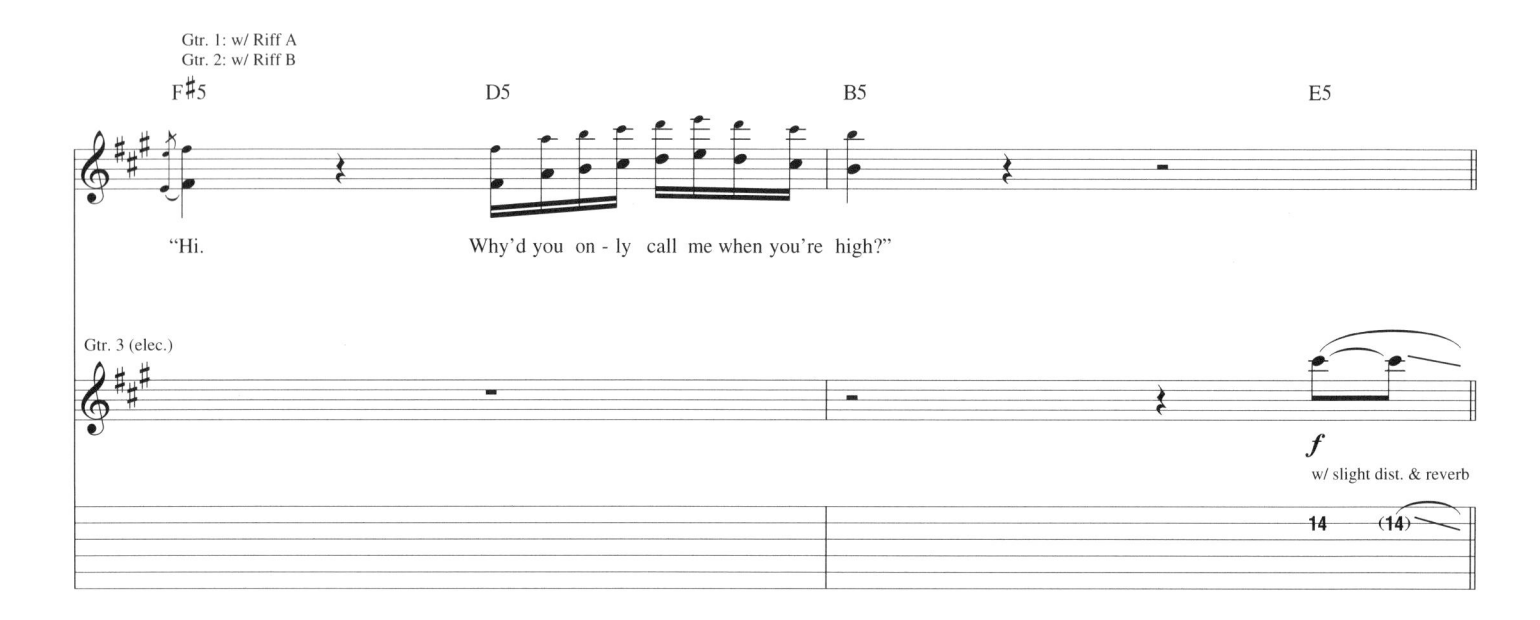

Verse

2. Some-where dark - er, talk-ing the same shite.

Gtr. 2: w/ Riff A
Gtrs. 3 & 4: w/ Riffs C & C1 (3 times)
F♯5
D5
B5
E5
I need a part - ner,
(High.)
well, "Are you out to - night?"
F♯5
D5
B5
E5
It's hard - er and hard - er to get you to lis - ten more I get through the gears.
Gtrs. 1 & 2
Riff D
End Riff D
P.M.
Gtrs. 1 & 2: w/ Riff A
F♯5
D5
B5
E5
In - ca - pa-ble of mak-ing al-right de - ci - sions, and hav-ing bad i - deas.
Chorus
Gtr. 1: w/ Riff D
Gtr. 2: w/ Riff B (3 times)
Gtr. 3: w/ Riff C (3 times)
F♯5
D5
B5
E5
Now, it's three in the morn - ing and I'm try-ing to change your
Gtr. 4
Riff E
End Riff E
P.M.

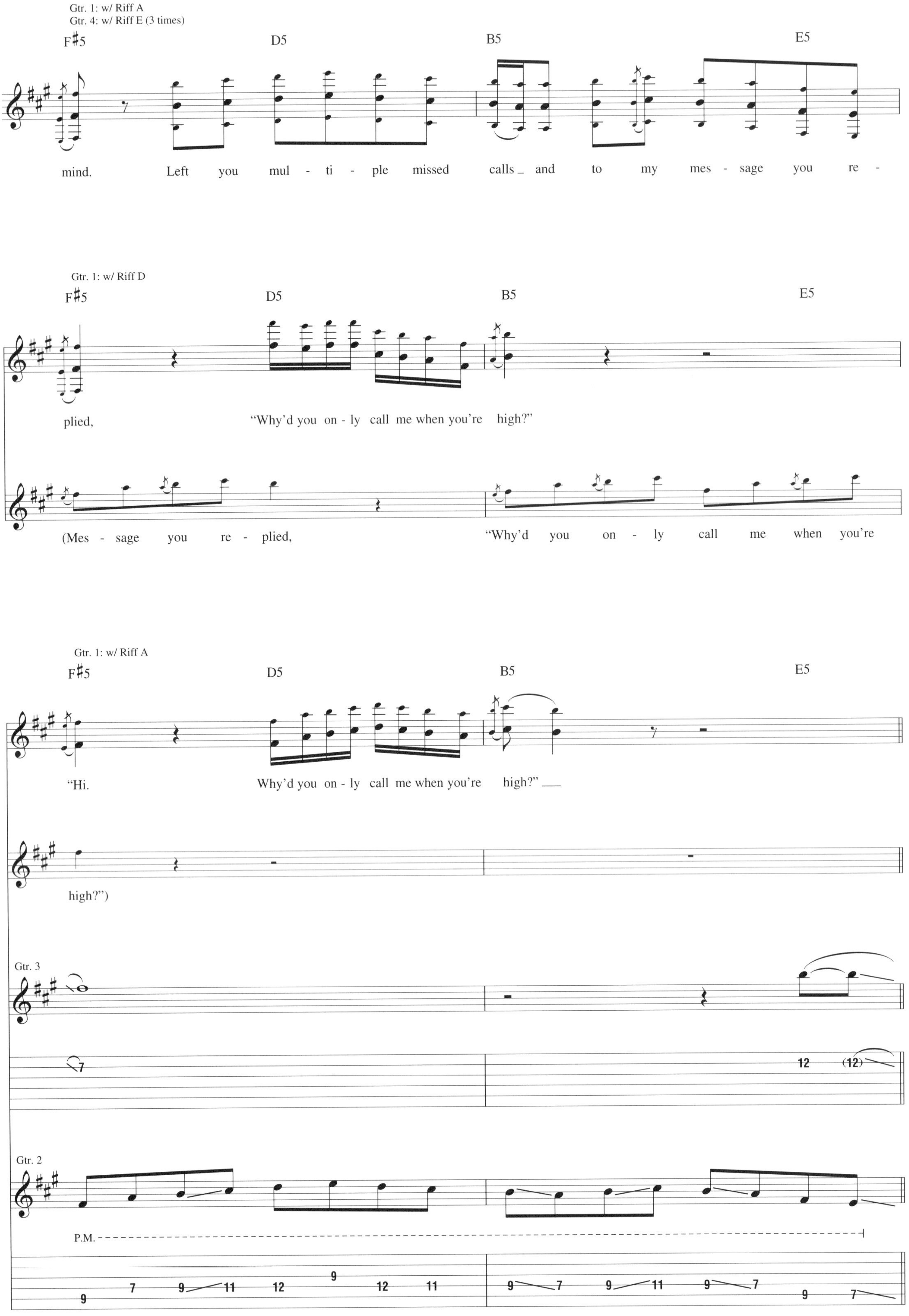
Gtr. 1: w/ Riff A
Gtr. 4: w/ Riff E (3 times)
F#5
D5
B5
E5
mind. Left you mul - ti - ple missed calls _ and to my mes - sage you re -
Gtr. 1: w/ Riff D
F#5
D5
B5
E5
plied, "Why'd you on - ly call me when you're high?"
(Mes - sage you re - plied, "Why'd you on - ly call me when you're
Gtr. 1: w/ Riff A
F#5
D5
B5
E5
"Hi. Why'd you on - ly call me when you're high?" ___
high?")
Gtr. 3
Gtr. 2
P.M.

Bridge

*(Am)   (C)   Gtr. 3 tacet   (Em)

And I can't see you here, wonder where I might.

*Symbols in parentheses represent chord names respective to capoed guitar.
See top of first page of song for chord diagrams pertaining to rhythm slashes.

**Top voice w/ echo set for quarter-note regeneration w/ 2 repeats.

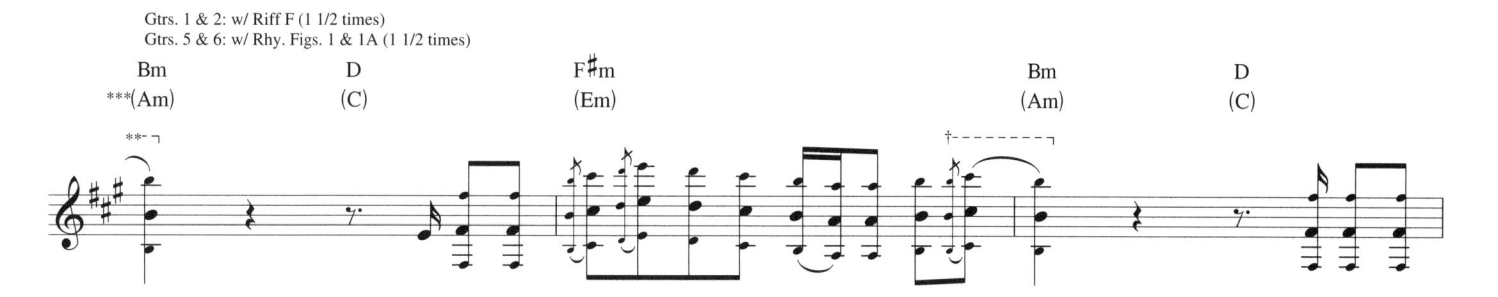

Gtrs. 1 & 2: w/ Riff F (1 1/2 times)
Gtrs. 5 & 6: w/ Rhy. Figs. 1 & 1A (1 1/2 times)

Bm   D   F#m   Bm   D
***(Am) (C) (Em)   (Am) (C)

It sorta feels like I'm running out of time.   I haven't

***Symbols in parentheses represent chord names respective to capoed guitar.
Symbols above represent actual sounding chords.

†As before

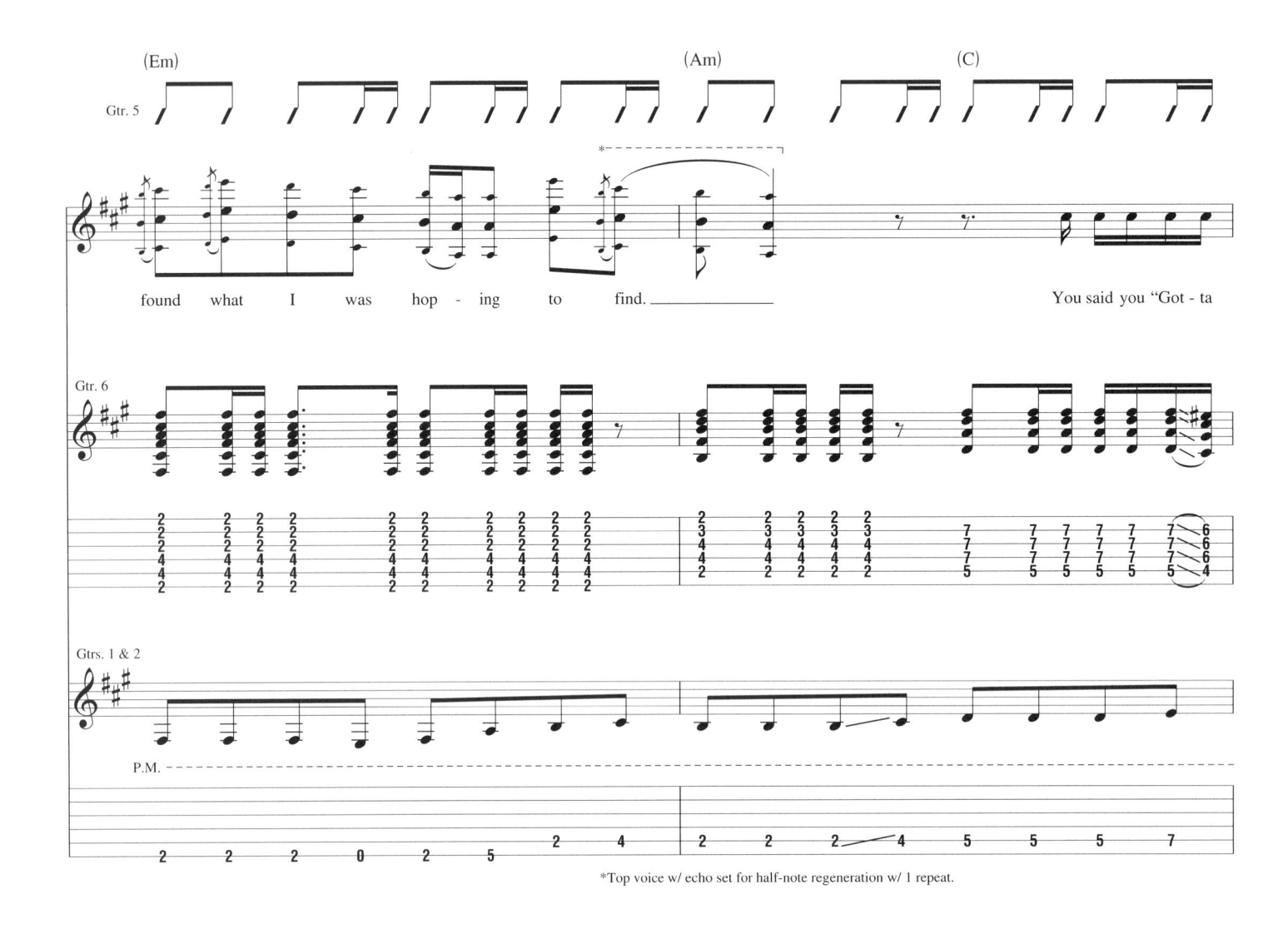

found what I was hop-ing to find. You said you "Got-ta be up in the morn-ing, gon-na have an ear-ly night." And "You're start-ing to bore me ba-by, why'd you on-ly call me when you're

*Top voice w/ echo set for half-note regeneration w/ 1 repeat.

**w/ slight dist. & octaver

**Octaver set for one octave above.

76

Interlude
Gtr. 5 tacet
D
F♯m
D
F♯m
Rhy. Fig. 2
End Rhy. Fig. 2
Gtr. 6
high?”
Gtr. 8 (elec.)
w/ slight dist.
Gtr. 7
Gtrs. 1 & 2
Riff G
End Riff G
P.M.
Gtrs. 1 & 2: w/ Riff G
Gtr. 6: w/ Rhy. Fig. 2
D
F♯m
D
F♯m
Why’d you
Gtr. 8
Gtr. 7

Outro

Lyrics:
only ever phone me when you're high? Why'd you only ever phone me when you're high? Why'd you only ever phone me when you're high? Why'd you only ever phone me when you're high?

Snap Out of It

Words by Alex Turner
Music by Arctic Monkeys

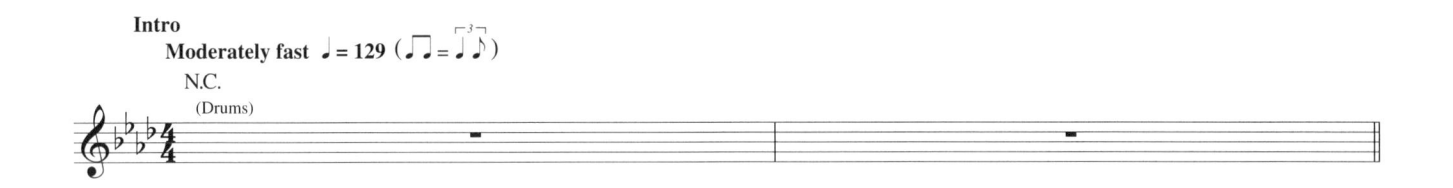

Intro
Moderately fast ♩ = 129
N.C. (Drums)

Verse
Chords: Fm — Fm(maj7) (repeating)

Lyric line 1: "1. What's been happening in your world?"

Rhy. Fig. 1 — Gtrs. 1 & 2, P.M. throughout

*Gtr. 1 (elec.) w/ clean tone, played *mf*; Gtr. 2 (acous.), played *mp*; composite arrangement.
**Chord symbols reflect overall harmony.

Lyric line 2: "What have you been up to?"

© 2013 EMI MUSIC PUBLISHING LTD.
All Rights in the U.S. and Canada Controlled and Administered by EMI APRIL MUSIC INC.
All Rights Reserved   International Copyright Secured   Used by Permission

Lyrics:

I heard that you fell in love ___ or near e-nough.

I got to tell you the truth, ___

Chorus

I want to grab both your shoul-ders and shake, ___ ba-by. Snap out of it. ___ (Snap out ___ of it.)

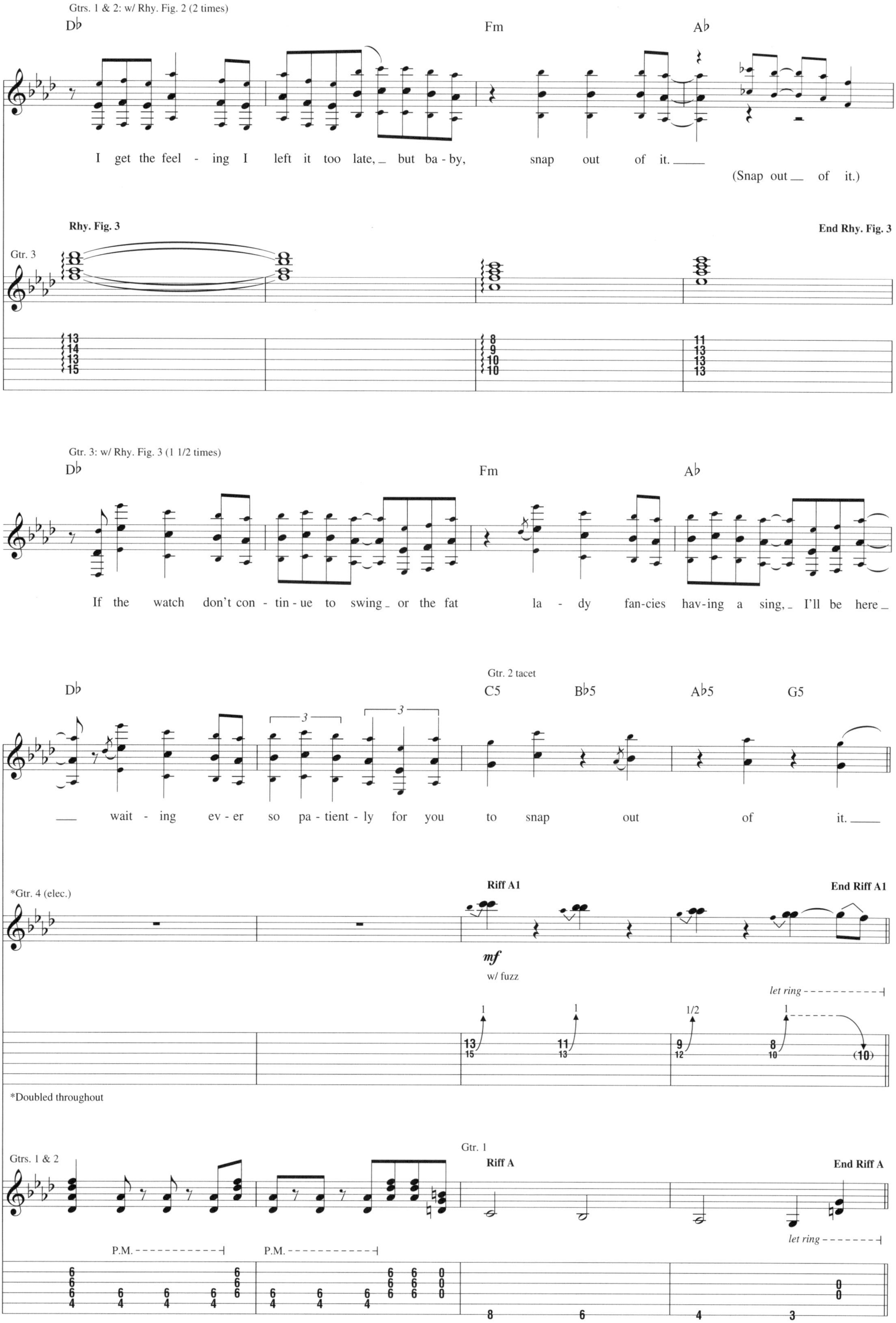

Gtrs. 1 & 2: w/ Rhy. Fig. 2 (2 times)
D♭
Fm
A♭
I get the feel - ing I left it too late, but ba - by, snap out of it.
(Snap out of it.)
Rhy. Fig. 3
End Rhy. Fig. 3
Gtr. 3
Gtr. 3: w/ Rhy. Fig. 3 (1 1/2 times)
D♭
Fm
A♭
If the watch don't con - tin - ue to swing or the fat la - dy fan-cies hav-ing a sing, I'll be here
D♭
Gtr. 2 tacet
C5
B♭5
A♭5
G5
waiting ev - er so pa - tient - ly for you to snap out of it.
*Gtr. 4 (elec.)
Riff A1
End Riff A1
mf
w/ fuzz
let ring
*Doubled throughout
Gtrs. 1 & 2
Gtr. 1
Riff A
End Riff A
let ring
P.M.
P.M.

Interlude

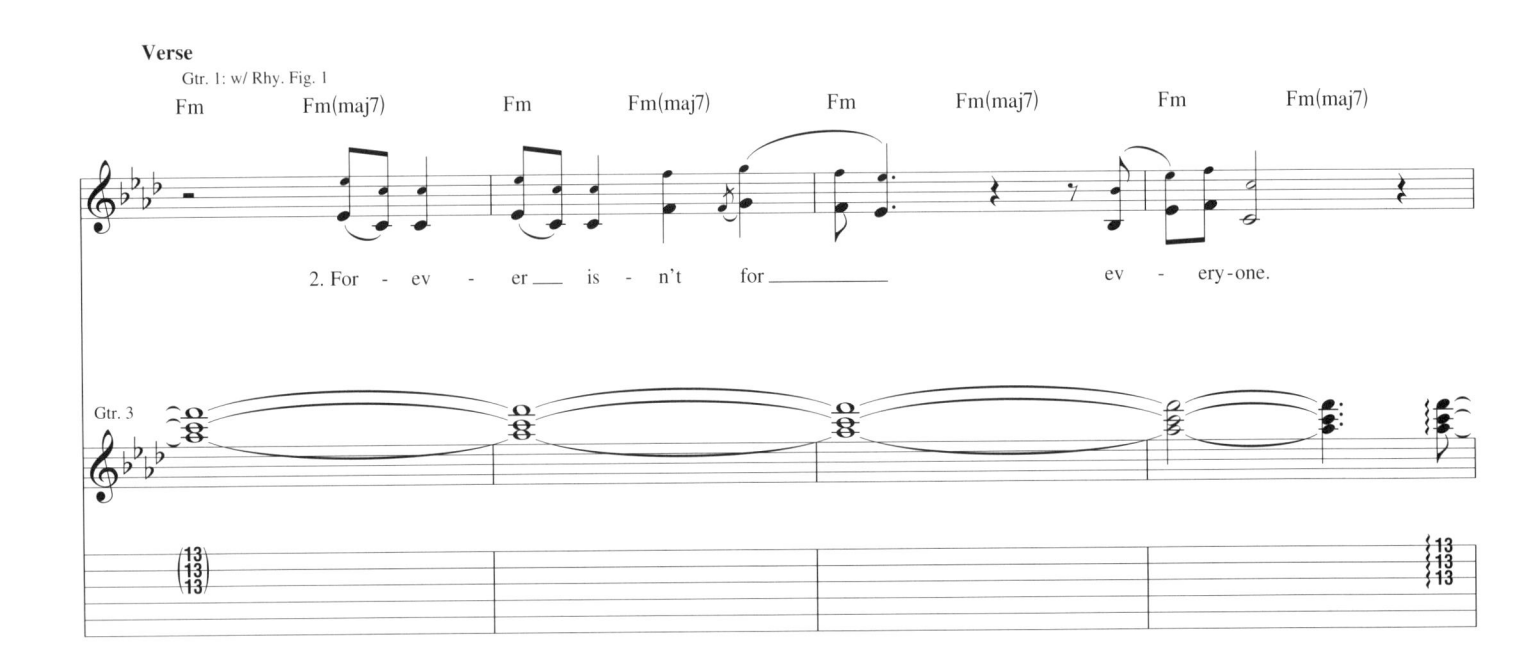

2. For-ev-er isn't for ev-ery-one.

Fm Fm(maj7) Fm Fm(maj7) Fm Fm(maj7) Fm Fm(maj7)
Is __ for - ev - er for you? ____
B♭m B♭m(maj7) B♭m7 B♭m6 B♭m B♭m(maj7) B♭m7 B♭m6
It sounds like set - tl - ing down ____ or giv-ing up. ____
8va
B♭m B♭m(maj7) B♭m7 B♭m6 B♭m B♭m(maj7) C
But it don't sound much like you ____ girl. ____
8va
Chorus
Gtr. 1: w/ Rhy. Fig. 2 (3 1/2 times)
Gtr. 3: w/ Rhy. Fig. 3 (3 1/2 times)
D♭ Fm A♭
I want to grab both your shoul-ders and shake, _ ba - by. Snap out of it. ____
(Snap out __ of it.)

Lyrics:

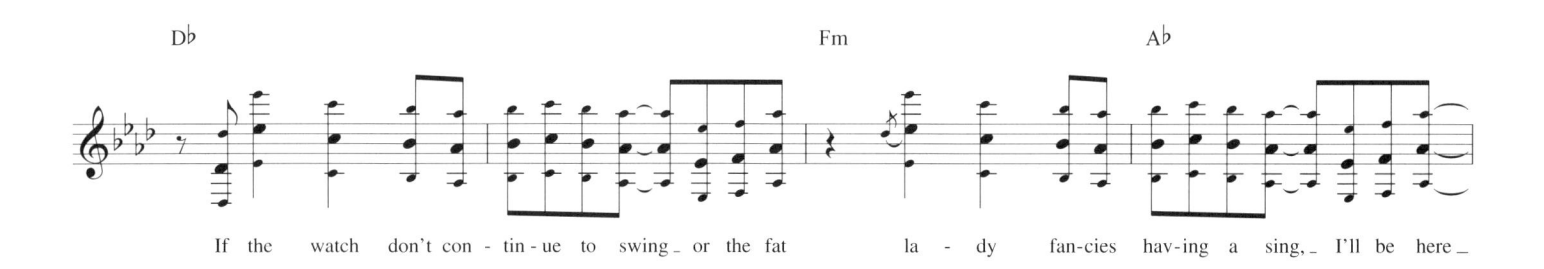

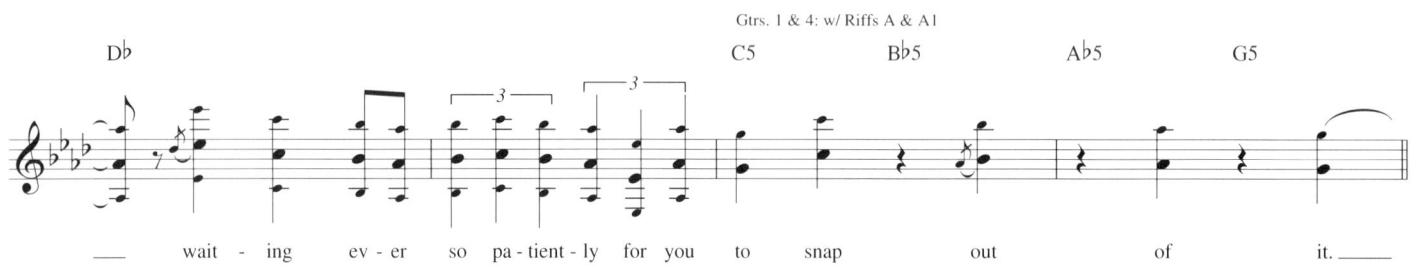

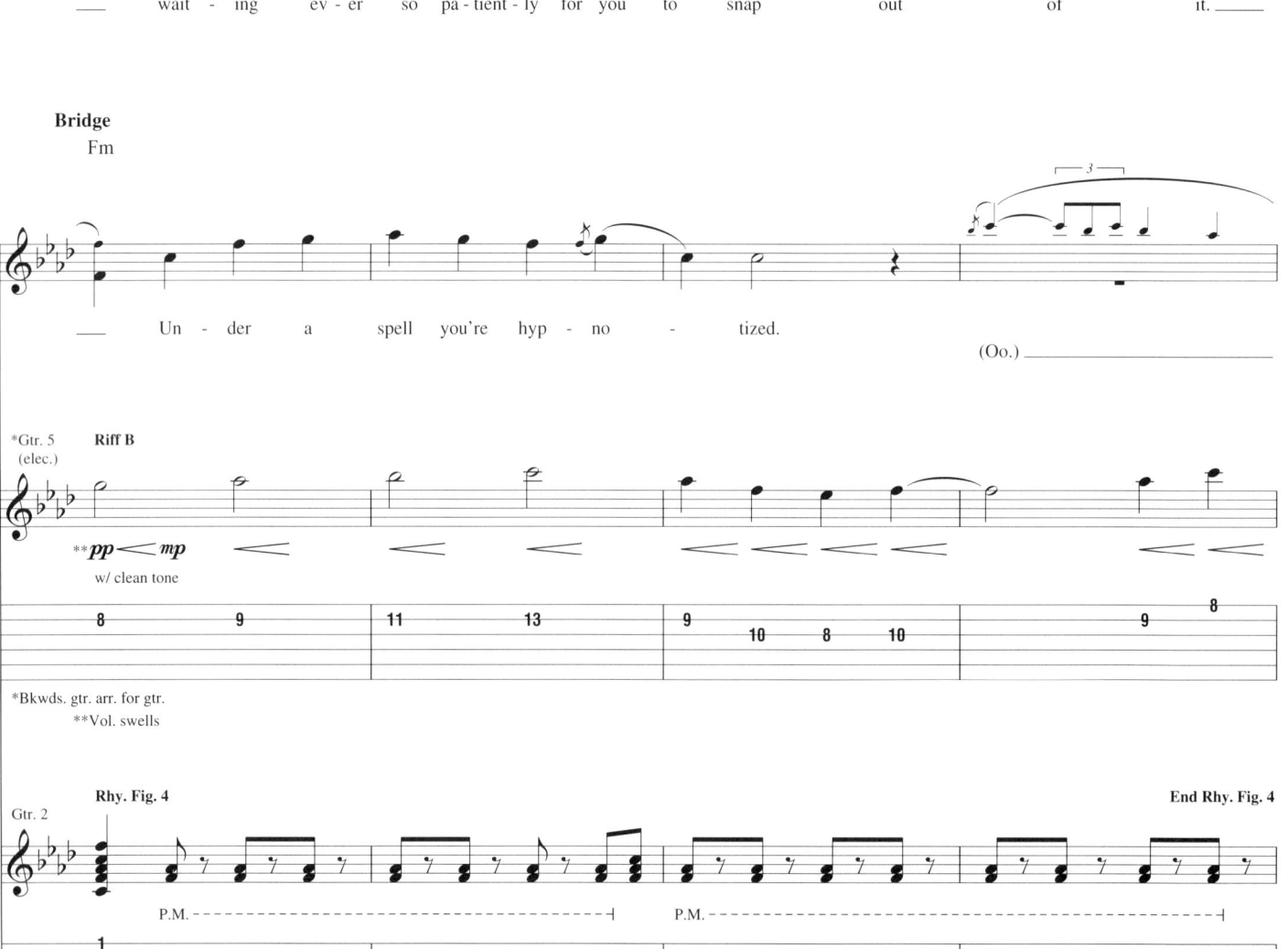

I get the feeling I left it too late, but baby, snap out of it. (Snap out of it.)

If the watch don't continue to swing or the fat lady fancies having a sing, I'll be here waiting ever so patiently for you to snap out of it.

Bridge

Under a spell you're hypnotized. (Oo.)

Darling, how could you be so blind? (Snap out of it.)

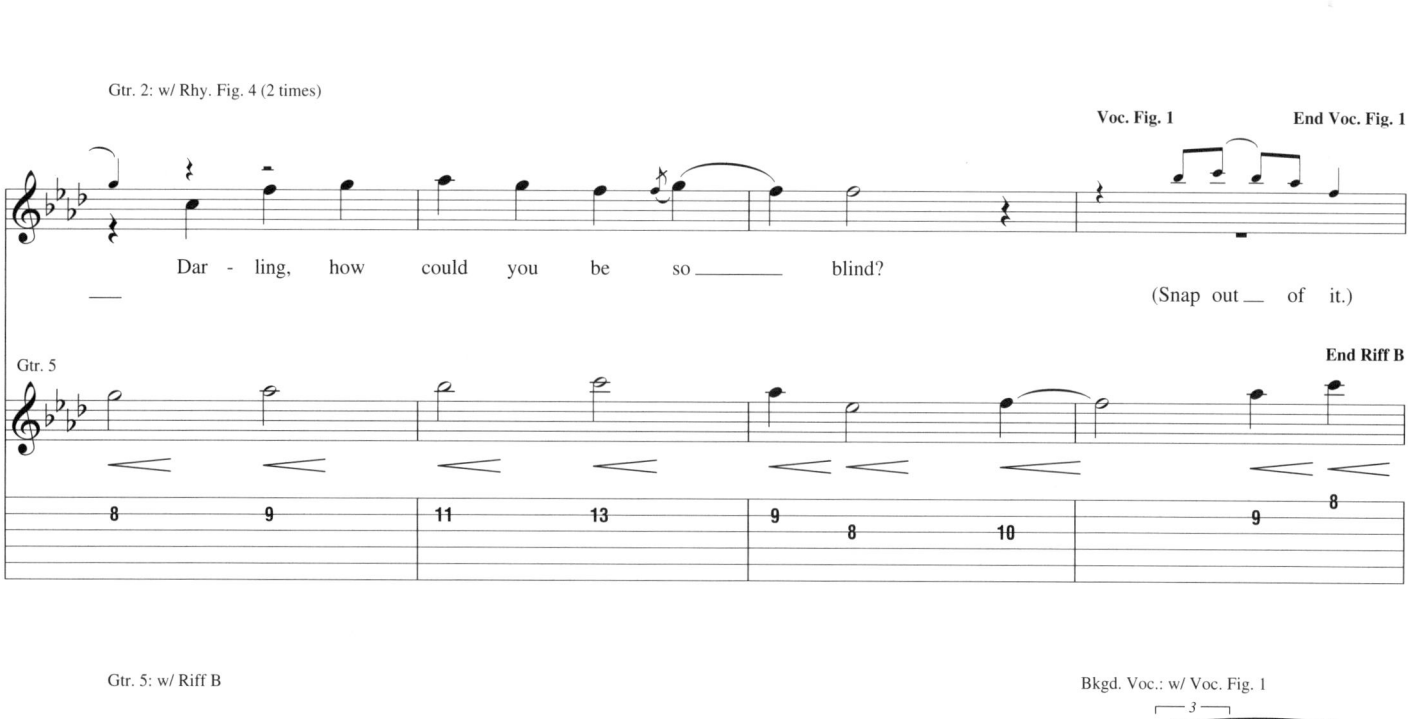

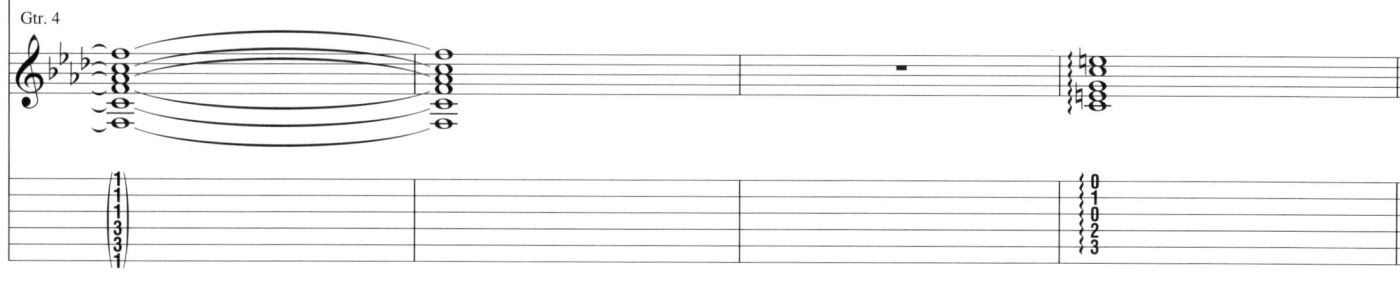

Under a spell you're hypnotized. (Oo.)

Darling, how could you be so blind?

Outro-Chorus

Gtrs. 1 & 2: w/ Rhy. Fig. 2 (3 1/2 times)
Gtr. 4 tacet
Gtr. 5: w/ Riff B (1 3/4 times)

Gtr. 3: w/ Rhy. Fig. 3 (last 2 meas.)

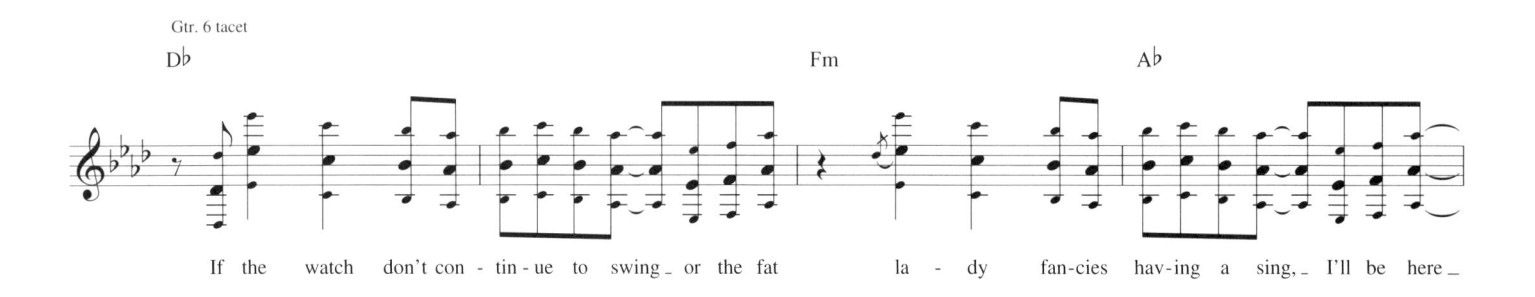

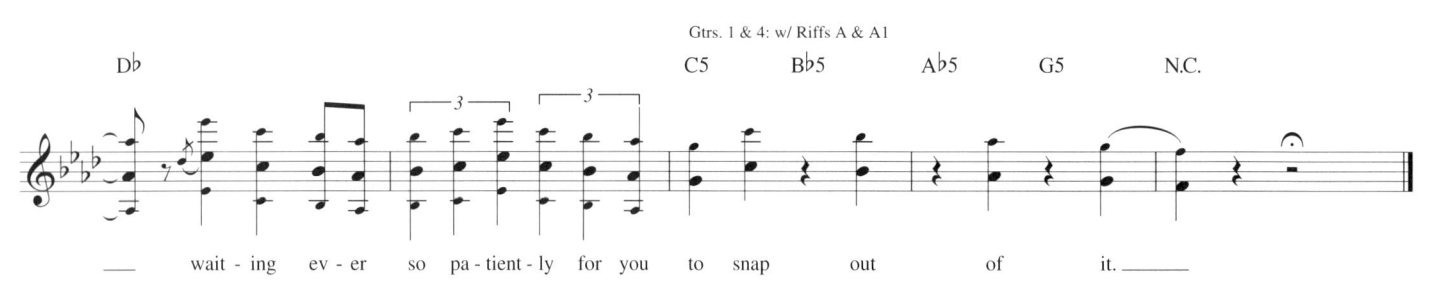

Db | Fm | Ab

I wan-na grab both your shoul-ders and shake, ba-by. Snap out of it.
(Snap out of it.)

Gtr. 6 (elec.)

*pp < mf
w/ dist.

*Vol. swells

Gtr. 3: w/ Rhy. Fig. 3 (2 1/2 times)

Db | Fm | Ab

I get the feel-ing I left it too late, but ba-by, snap out of it.
(Snap out of it.)

Gtr. 6 tacet

Db | Fm | Ab

If the watch don't con-tin-ue to swing or the fat la-dy fan-cies hav-ing a sing, I'll be here

Gtrs. 1 & 4: w/ Riffs A & A1

Db | C5 | Bb5 | Ab5 | G5 | N.C.

wait-ing ev-er so pa-tient-ly for you to snap out of it.

Knee Socks

Words by Alex Turner
Music by Arctic Monkeys

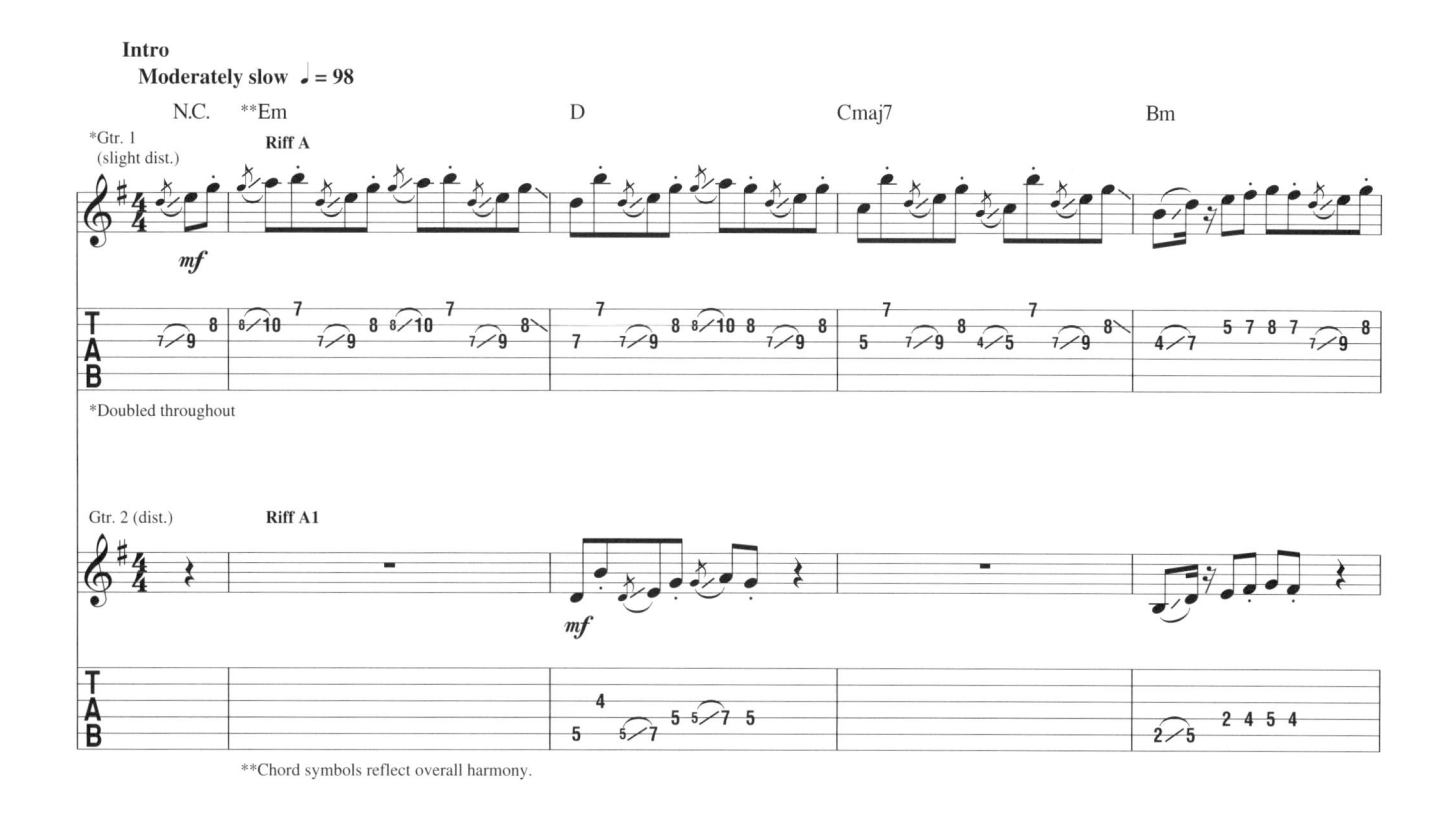

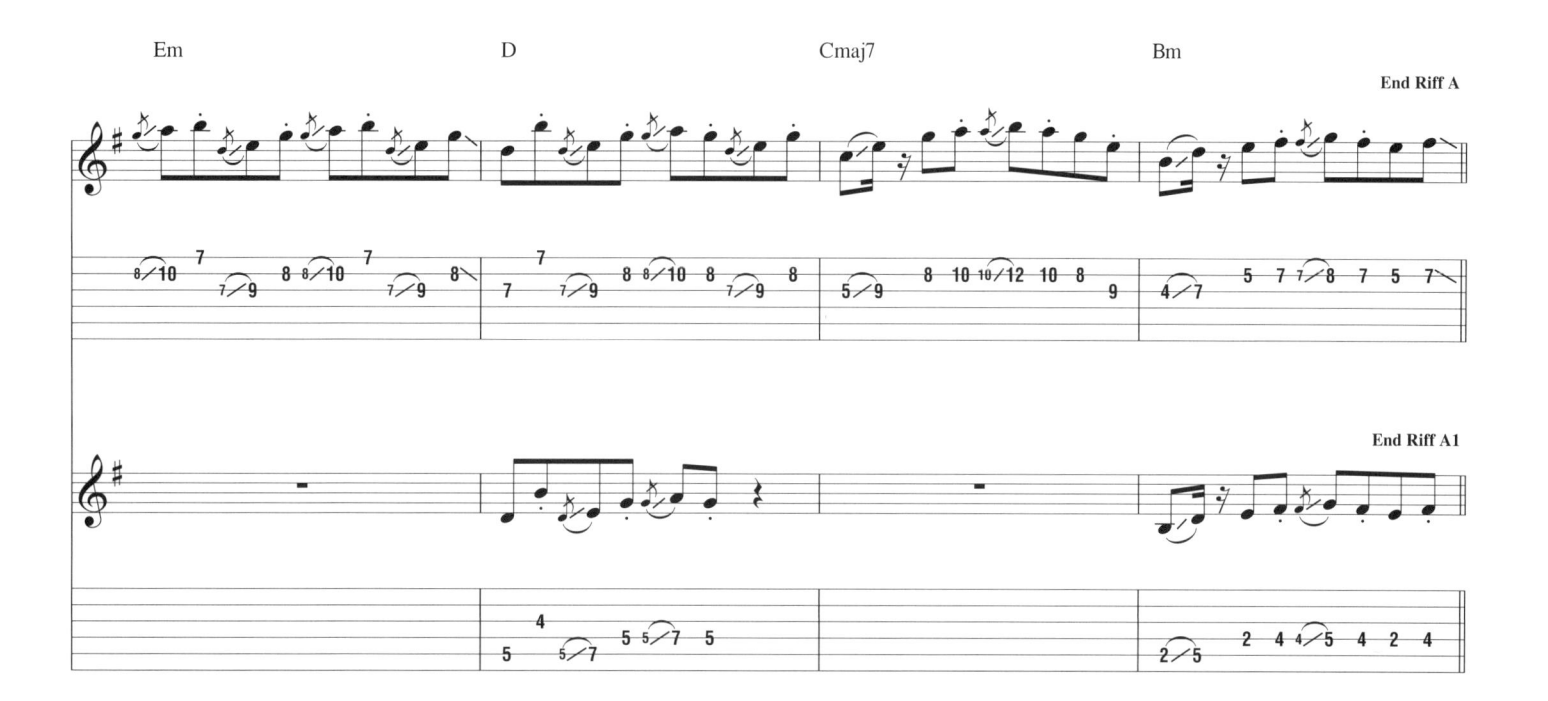

Intro
Moderately slow ♩ = 98

*Doubled throughout

**Chord symbols reflect overall harmony.

© 2013 EMI MUSIC PUBLISHING LTD.
All Rights in the U.S. and Canada Controlled and Administered by EMI APRIL MUSIC INC.
All Rights Reserved   International Copyright Secured   Used by Permission

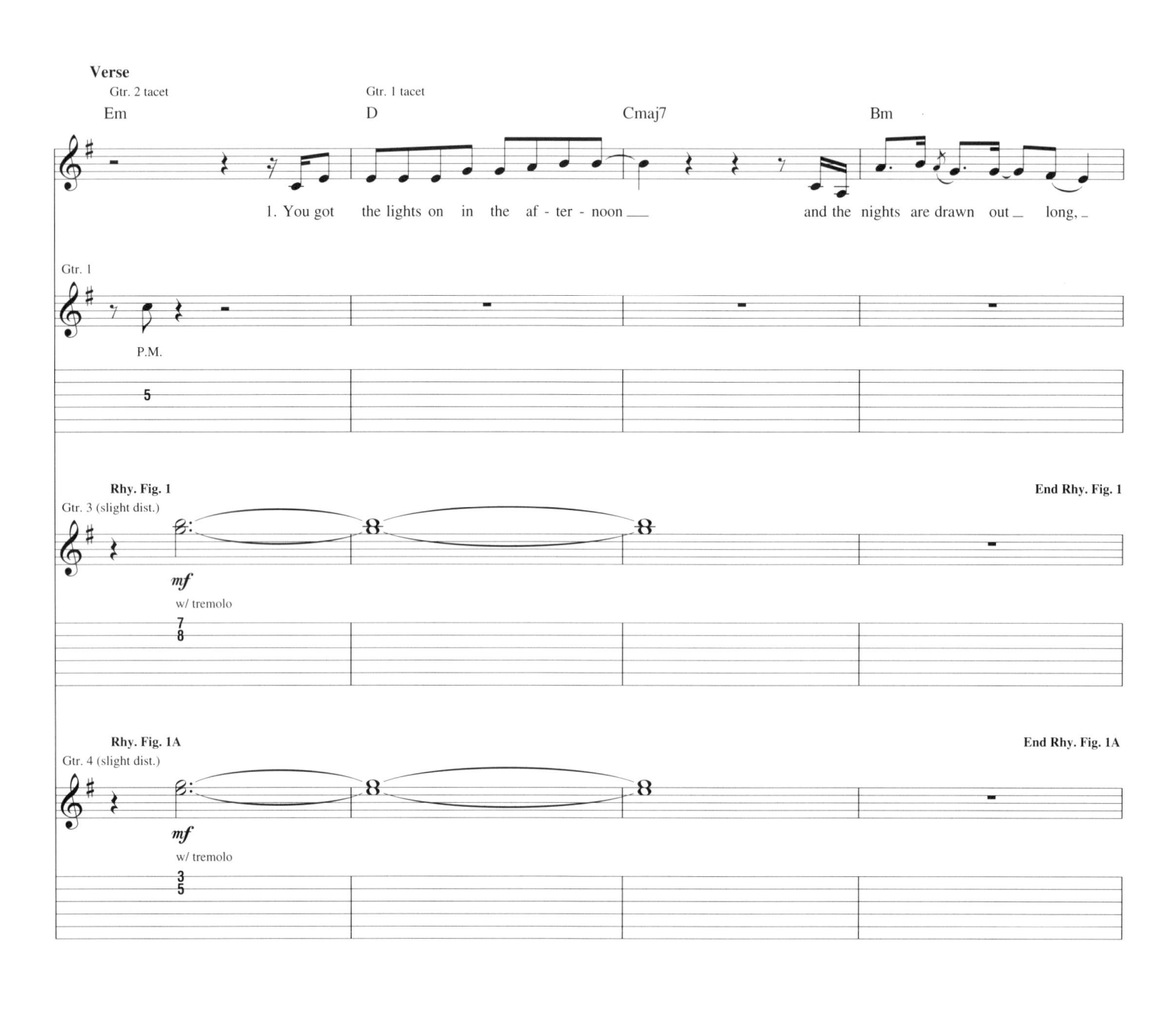

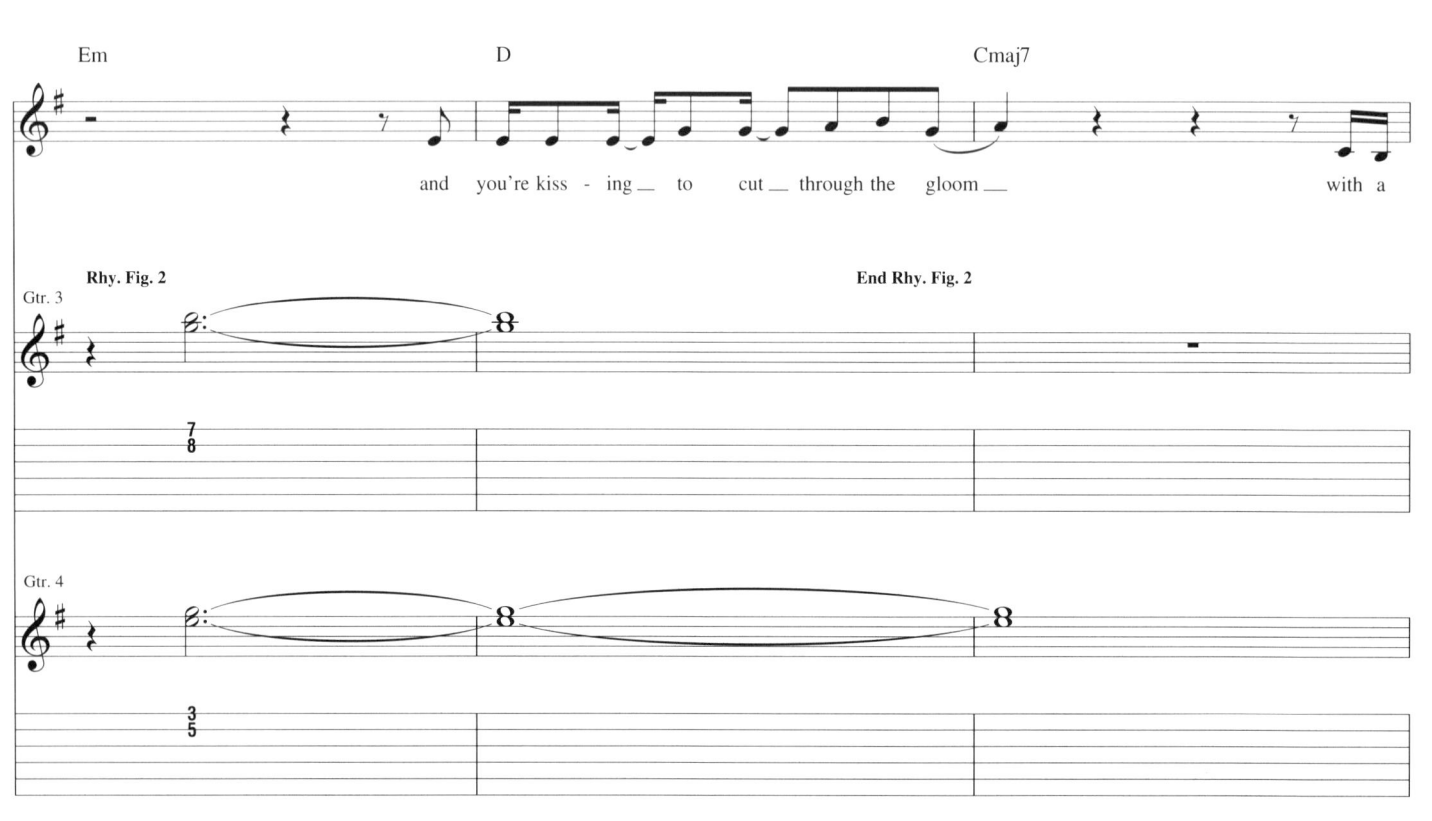

Verse

| Em | D | Cmaj7 | Bm |

1. You got the lights on in the af-ter-noon __ and the nights are drawn out __ long, __

Gtr. 1
P.M.

Rhy. Fig. 1 — Gtr. 3 (slight dist.) — *mf* w/ tremolo — **End Rhy. Fig. 1**

Rhy. Fig. 1A — Gtr. 4 (slight dist.) — *mf* w/ tremolo — **End Rhy. Fig. 1A**

| Em | D | Cmaj7 |

and you're kiss-ing __ to cut __ through the gloom __ with a

Rhy. Fig. 2 — Gtr. 3 — **End Rhy. Fig. 2**

Gtr. 4

88

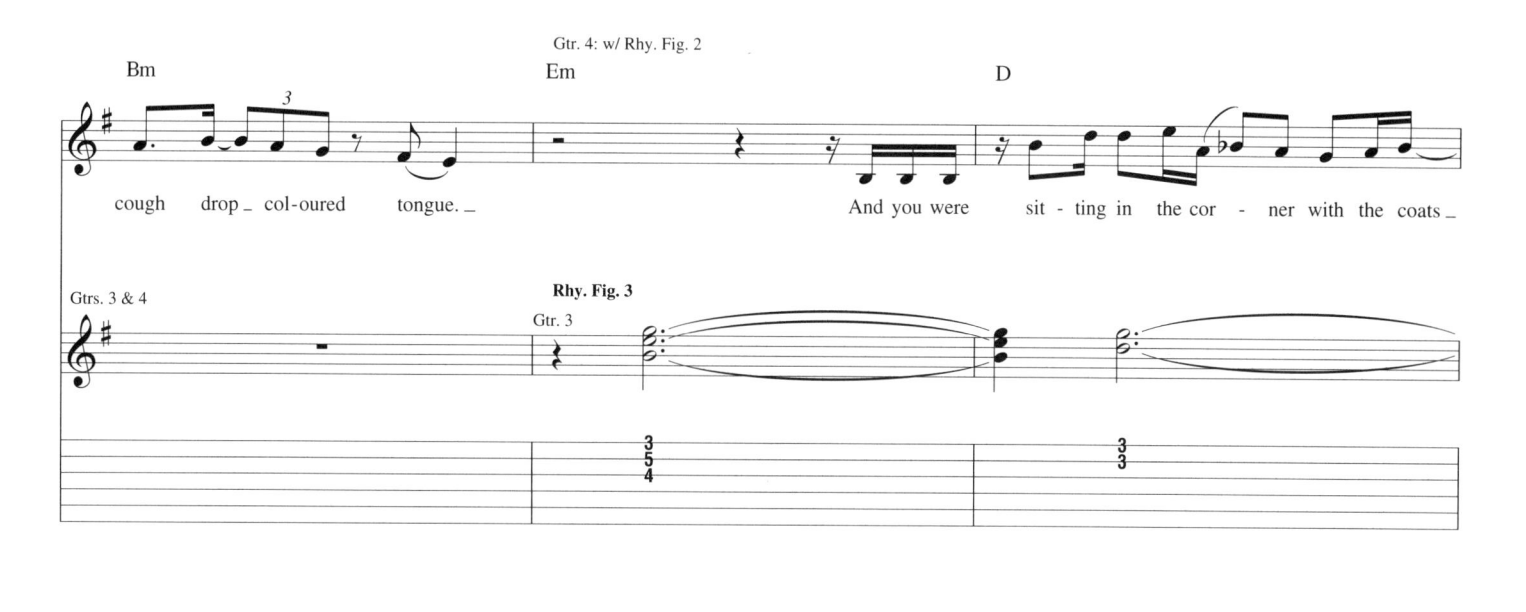

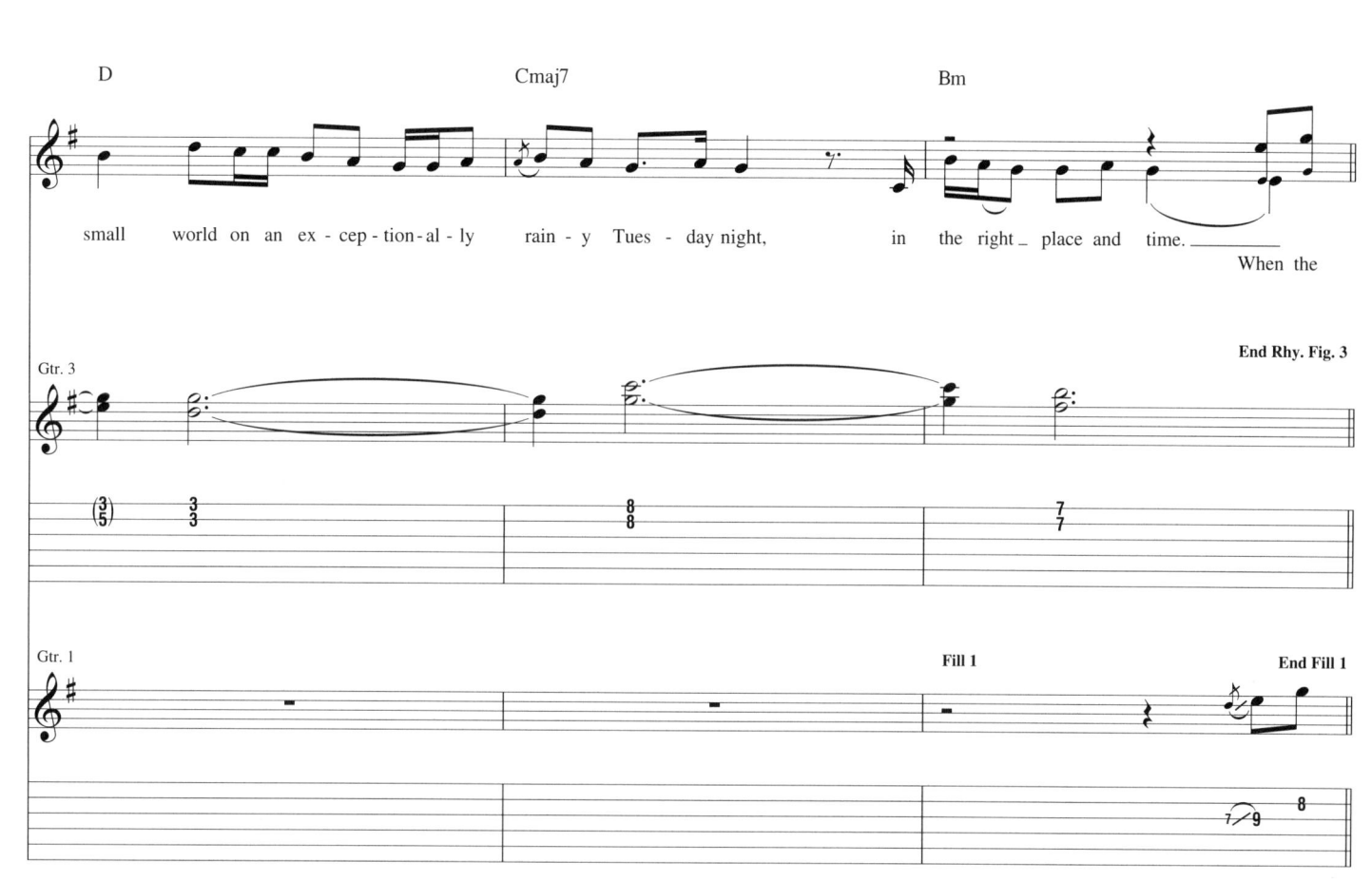

cough drop coloured tongue. And you were sitting in the corner with the coats all piled high and I thought you might be mine. In a small world on an exceptionally rainy Tuesday night, in the right place and time. When the

Chorus

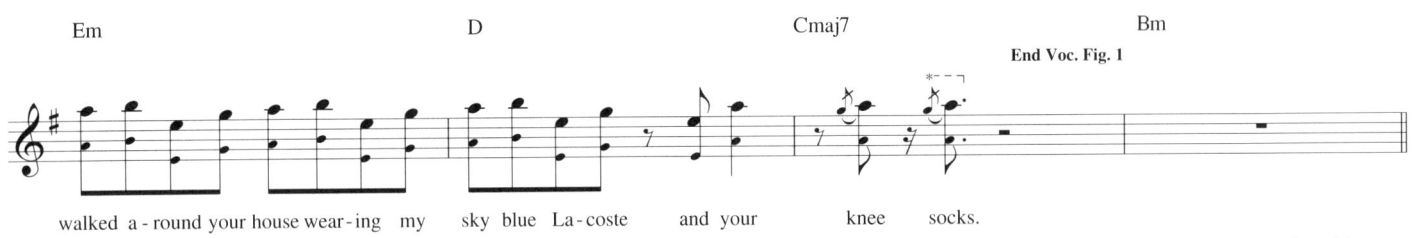

Gtrs. 1 & 2: w/ Riffs A & A1
Gtrs. 3 & 4: w/ Rhy. Figs. 1 & 1A (2 times)

Voc. Fig. 1

| Em | D | Cmaj7 | Bm |

ze - ros line up on the twen-ty - four hour clock. When you know who's call-ing e - ven though the num-ber is blocked. When you

| Em | D | Cmaj7 | Bm |

End Voc. Fig. 1

walked a - round your house wear-ing my sky blue La-coste and your knee socks.

*Ld. Voc.: w/ echo set for dotted eighth-note regeneration w/ 6 repeats.

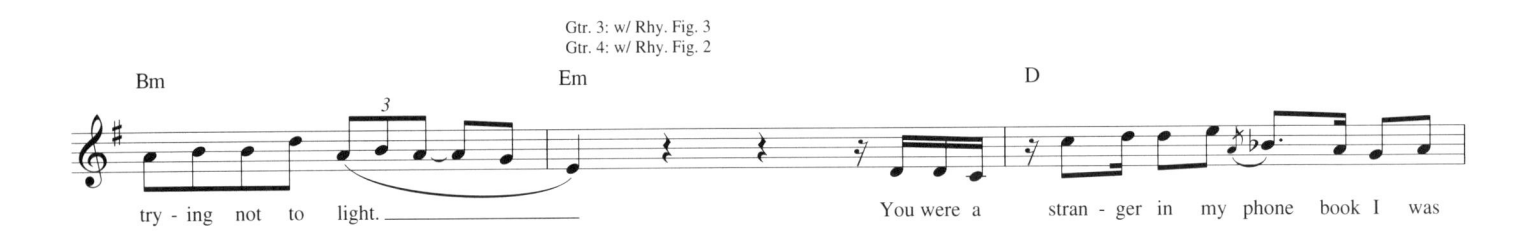

Verse

Gtrs. 3 & 4: w/ Rhy. Figs. 1 & 1A
Gtr. 1 tacet

| Em | D | Cmaj7 | Bm |

2. Well, you cured my Jan-u-ar-y blues. Yeah, you made it all al-right.

Gtr. 1

| Em | D | Cmaj7 |

I got a feel-ing I might have lit the ver-y fuse that you were

Gtr. 3: w/ Rhy. Fig. 3
Gtr. 4: w/ Rhy. Fig. 2

| Bm | Em | D |

try-ing not to light. You were a stran-ger in my phone book I was

Gtr. 4: w/ Rhy. Fig. 2

| Cmaj7 | Bm | Em |

act-ing like I knew 'cause I had noth-ing to lose. When the

[Verse]

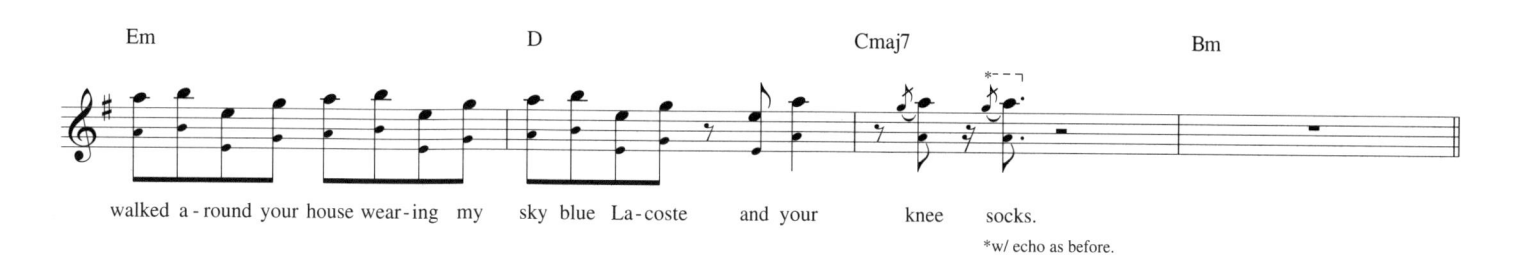

D | Cmaj7 | Bm

winter is in __ full swing __ and your __ dreams just aren't __ com-ing true, ain't it fun-ny what you'll __ do? __
When the

Chorus

Gtrs. 1 & 2: w/ Riffs A & A1
Gtrs. 3 & 4: w/ Rhy. Figs. 1 & 1A (2 times)

Em | D | Cmaj7 | Bm

ze-ros line up on the twen-ty-four hour __ clock. When you know who's call-ing e-ven though the num-ber is blocked. When you

Em | D | Cmaj7 | Bm

walked a-round your house wear-ing my sky blue La-coste and your knee socks.

*w/ echo as before.

Bridge

Am | C | Em

The late af-ter-noon, the ghost in your room that you al-ways thought did-n't ap-prove of you

Gtr. 1

Gtr. 2

Gtrs. 3 & 4

91

D | C | B5

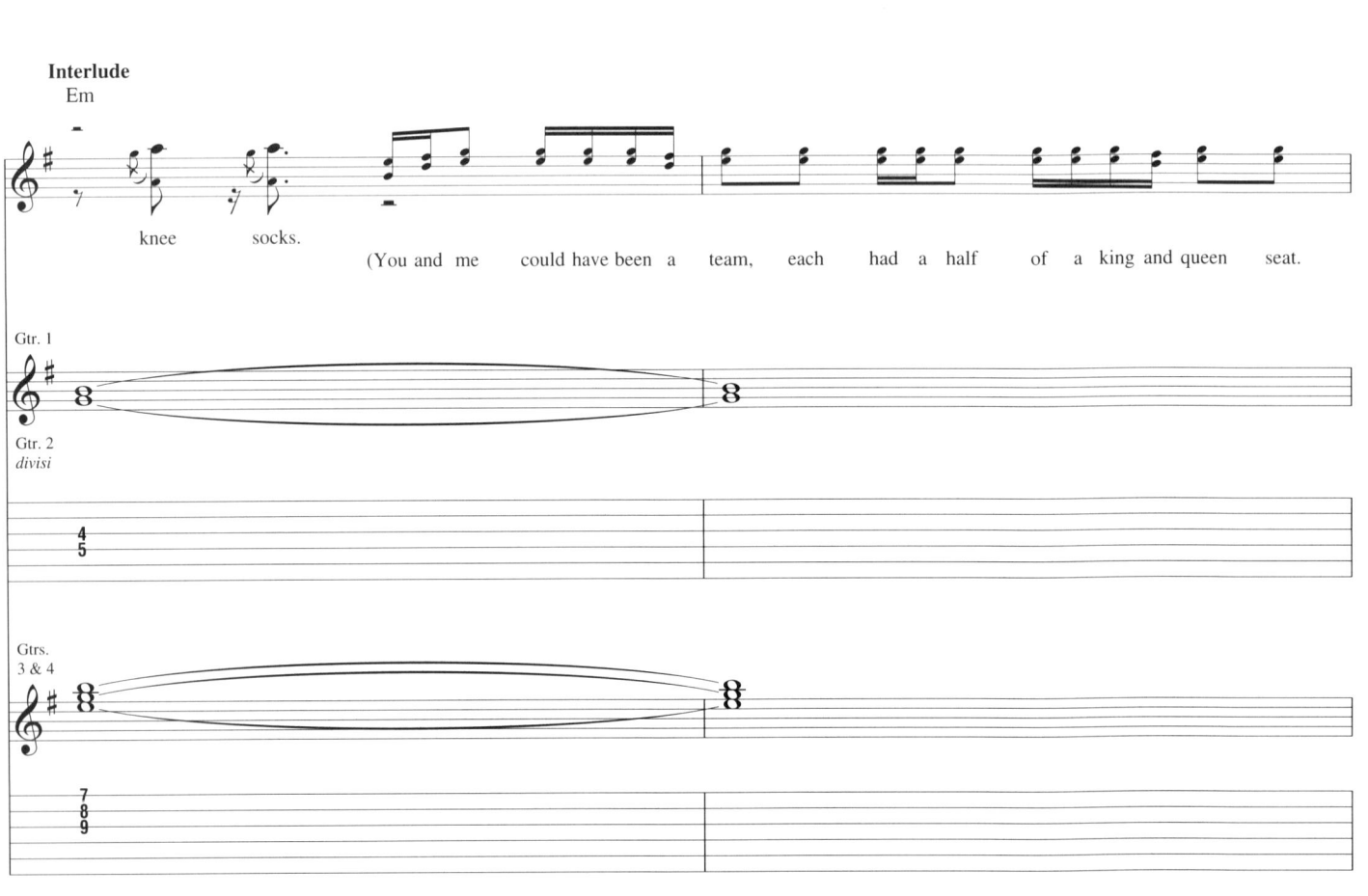

knock-ing boots. Nev-er stopped you let-ting me get hold of the sweet spot by the scruff of your

Interlude
Em

knee socks. (You and me could have been a team, each had a half of a king and queen seat.

Gtr. 1

Gtr. 2
divisi

Gtrs. 3 & 4

Gtrs. 1-4 tacet

Like the be-gin-ning of Mean Streets, you could Be My Ba - by.

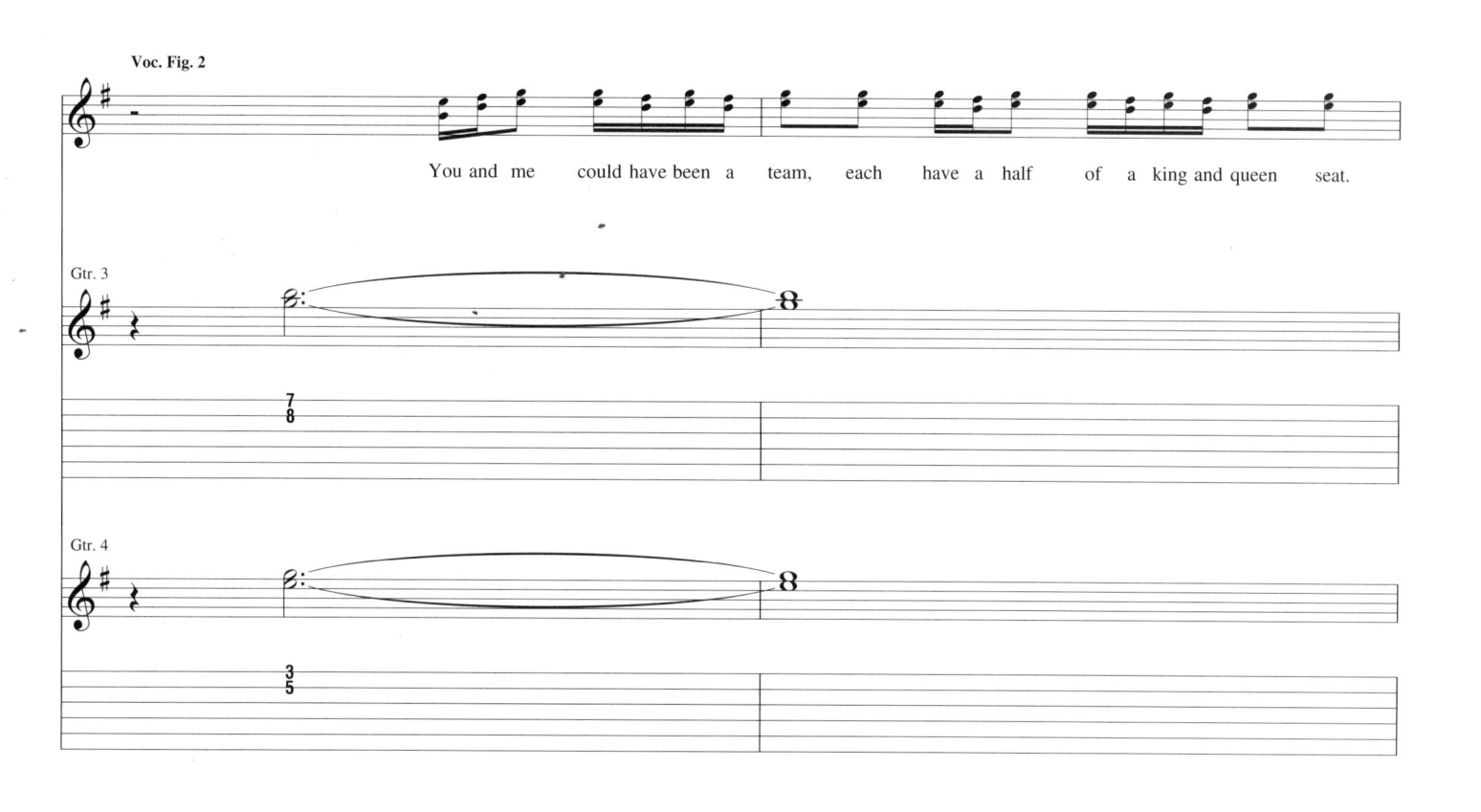

*w/ echo set for half-note regeneration w/ 1 repeat.

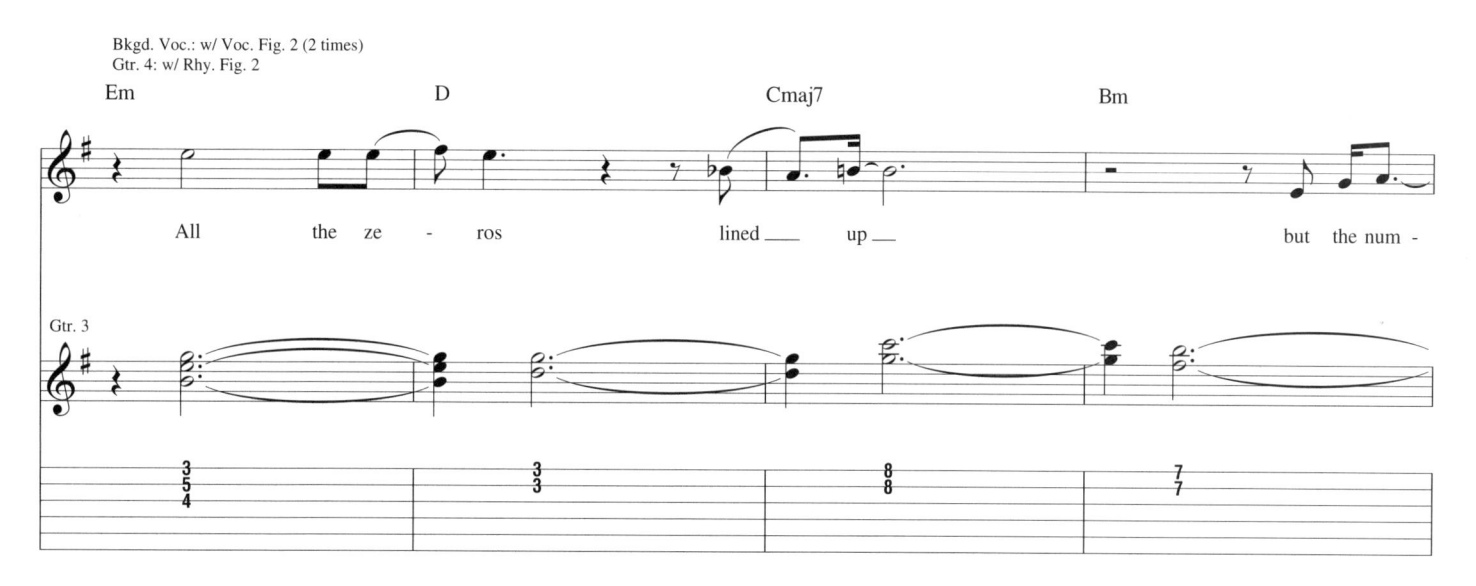

Voc. Fig. 2

You and me could have been a team, each have a half of a king and queen seat.

Gtr. 3

Gtr. 4

Gtrs. 3 & 4 tacet

End Voc. Fig. 2

Like the be-gin-ning of Mean Streets, you could Be My Ba - by.)

**As before

Bkgd. Voc.: w/ Voc. Fig. 2 (2 times)
Gtr. 4: w/ Rhy. Fig. 2

| Em | D | Cmaj7 | Bm |

All the ze - ros lined up but the num -

Gtr. 3

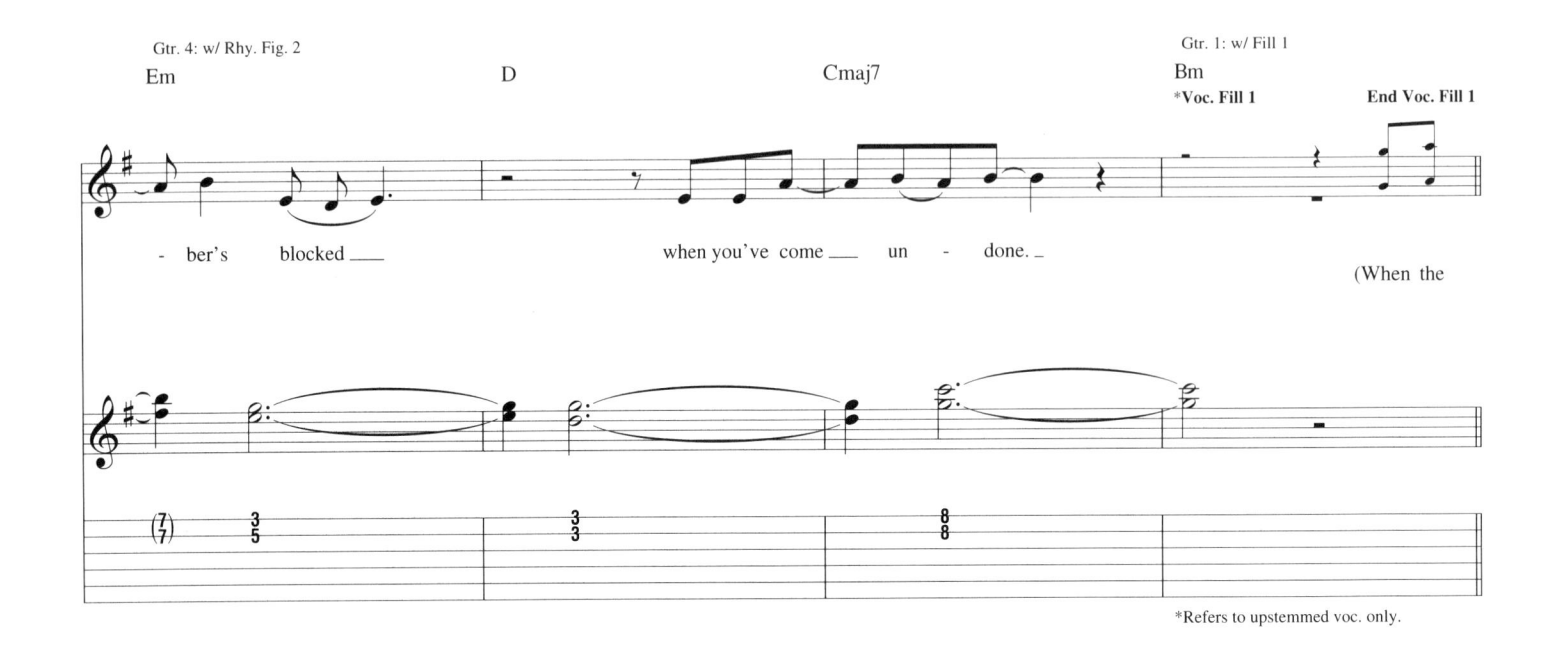

Gtr. 4: w/ Rhy. Fig. 2
Gtr. 1: w/ Fill 1

Em D Cmaj7 Bm

*Voc. Fill 1 End Voc. Fill 1

-ber's blocked ___ when you've come ___ un - done. ___

(When the

*Refers to upstemmed voc. only.

Chorus
Bkgd. Voc.: w/ Voc. Fig. 1
Gtrs. 1 & 2: w/ Riffs A & A1 (2 times)

Em D Cmaj7 Bm

All the ze - ros lined ___ up ___ but the num-

**Gtrs. 3 & 4

**Composite arrangement

Bkgd. Voc.: w/ Voc. Fill 1

Em D Cmaj7 Bm

-ber's blocked ___ when you've come ___ un - done.

Bkgd. Voc.: w/ Voc. Fig. 1
Gtrs. 3 & 4: w/ Rhy. Fig. 3

All the ze - ros lined up

Gtr. 5 (12-str. elec.)

mf
w/ clean tone & phaser

Outro

Gtrs. 3 & 4: w/ Rhy. Figs. 1 & 1A   Gtr. 5 tacet

Knee socks.

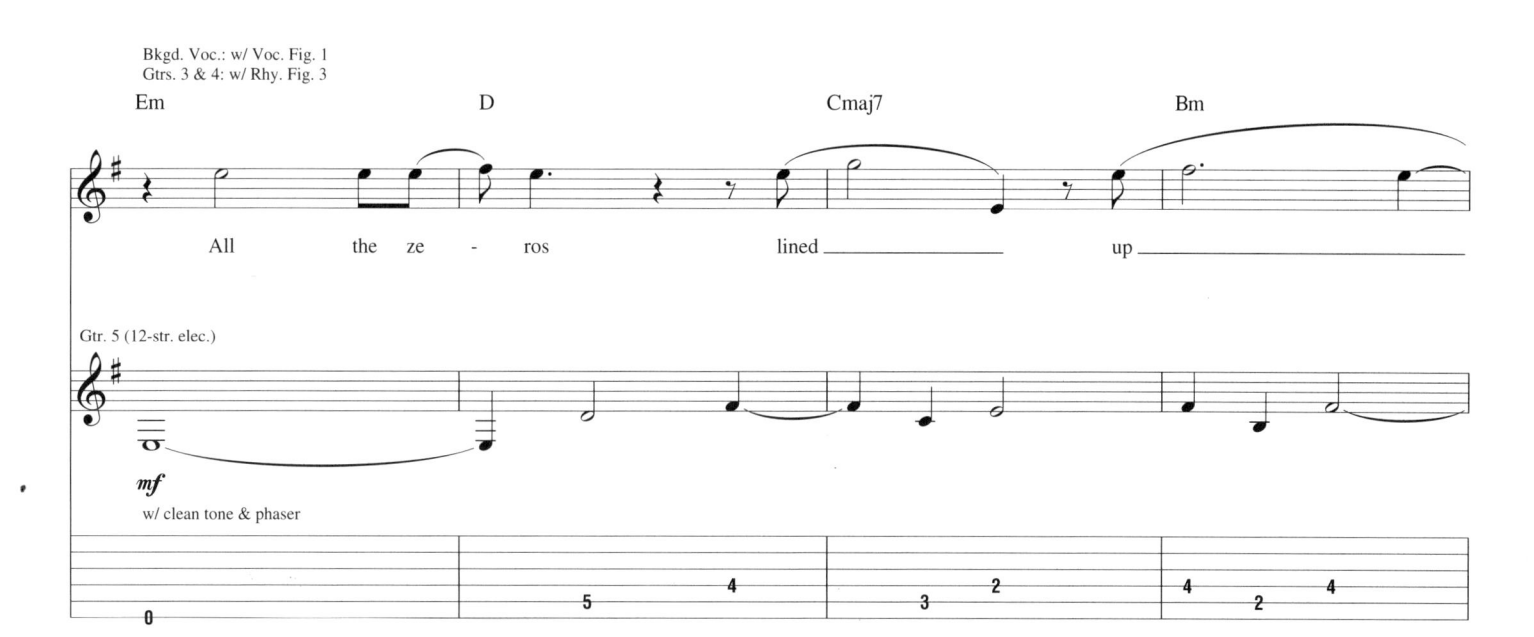

*Ld. Voc.: w/ echo set for dotted eighth-note regeneration w/ 6 repeats.

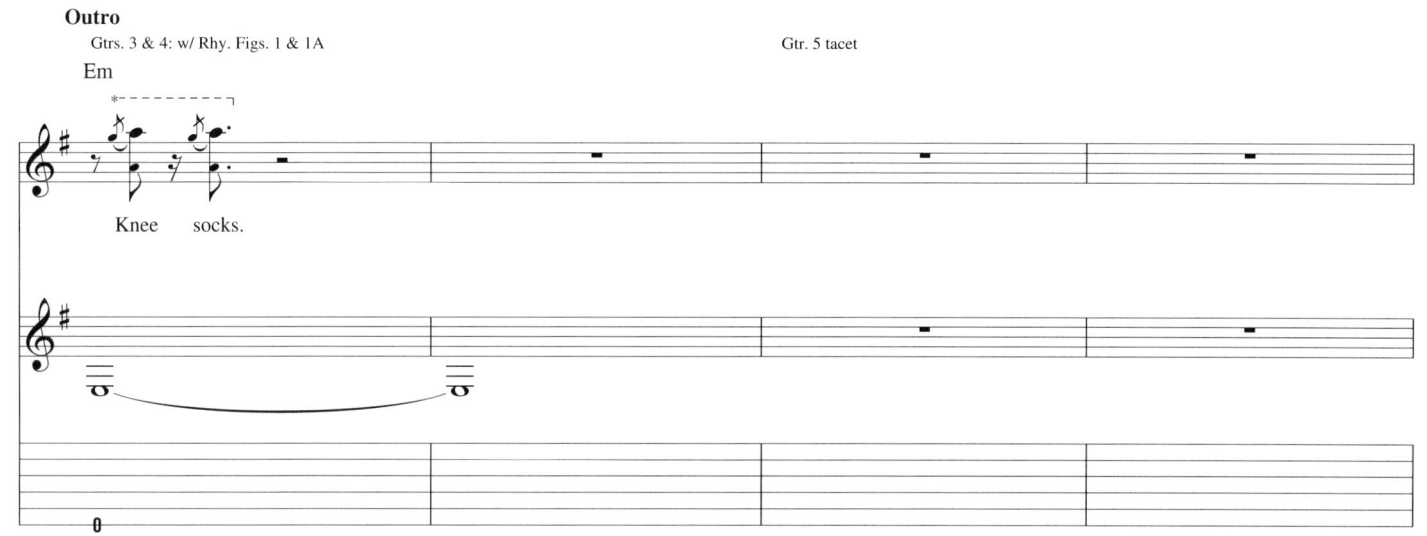

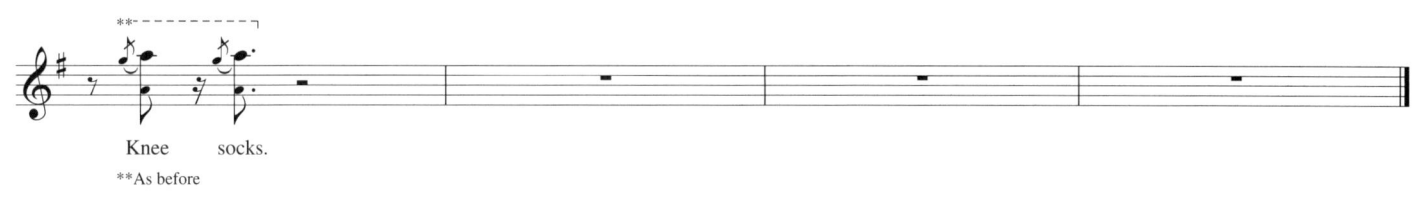

Knee socks.

**As before

I Wanna Be Yours

Words by Alex Turner and John Cooper Clarke
Music by Arctic Monkeys

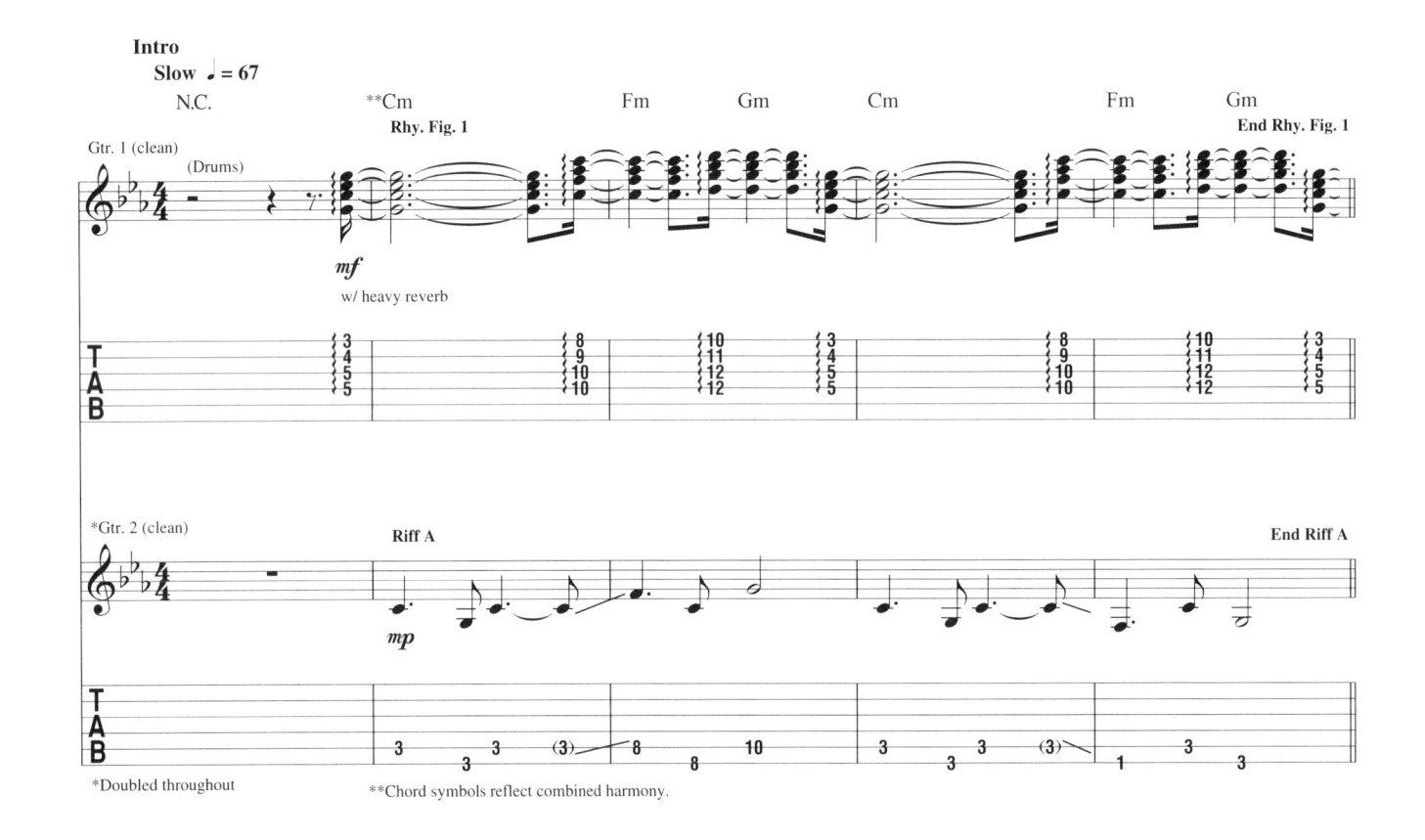

*Doubled throughout
**Chord symbols reflect combined harmony.

1. I wan-na be your vac-uum clean-er, breath-ing in your dust. I wan-na be your Ford Cor-ti-na, I _____ won't ev-er rust. _____ If you like your cof-fee hot, _____ let me be your cof-fee pot.

© 2013 EMI Music Publishing Ltd. and EMI Songs Ltd.
All Rights for EMI Music Publishing Ltd. in the U.S. and Canada Controlled and Administered by EMI April Music Inc.
All Rights for EMI Songs Ltd. in the U.S. and Canada Controlled and Administered by EMI Blackwood Music Inc.
All Rights Reserved   International Copyright Secured   Used by Permission

Cm ... **Fm** ... **Gm**

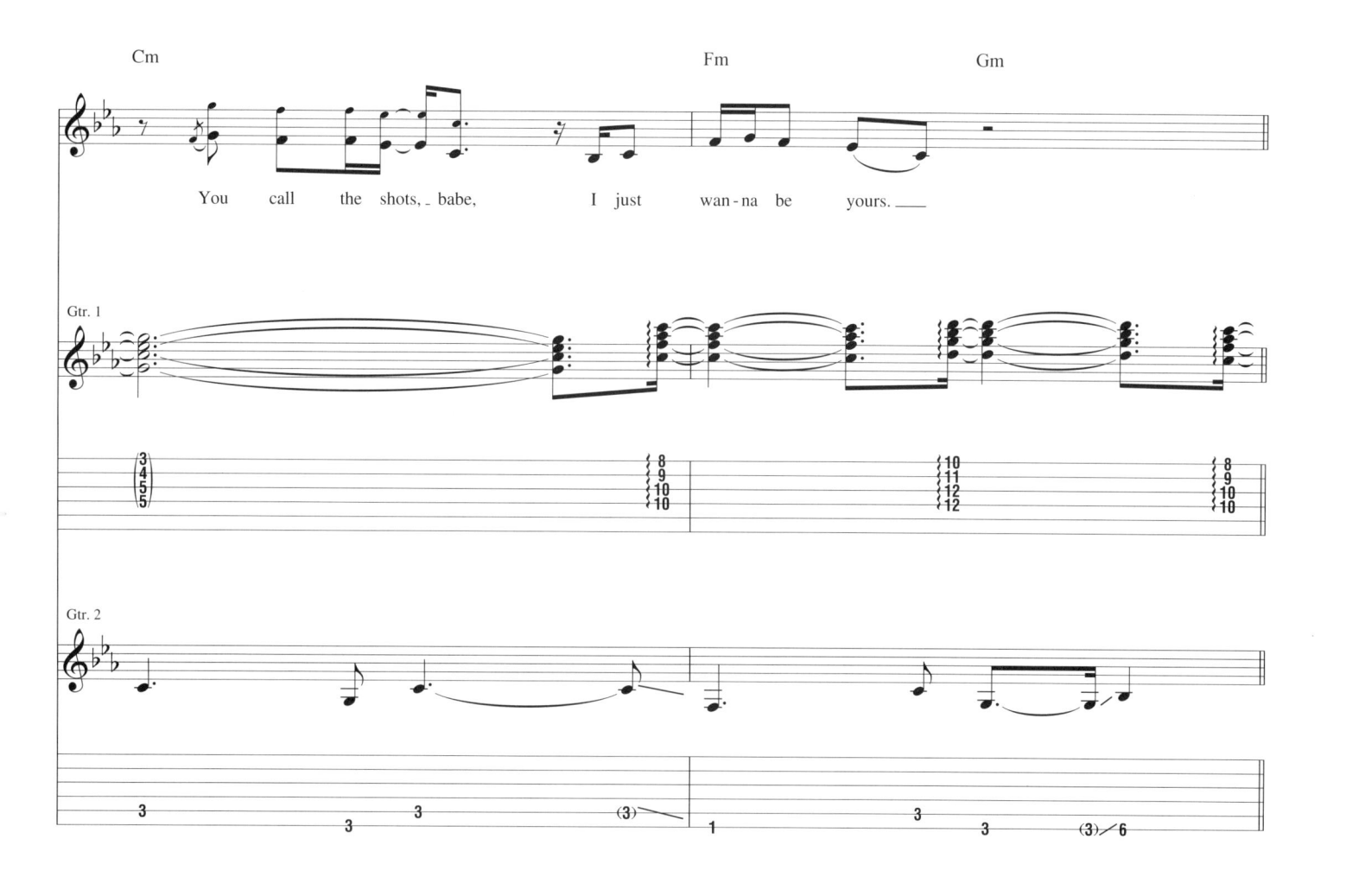

You call the shots, babe, I just wanna be yours.

Pre-Chorus

Fm ... **Gm** ... **Cm** ... **Fm** ... **Gm**

Se-crets I have held in my heart are hard-er to hide than I thought. May-be I just wan-na be yours, I

98

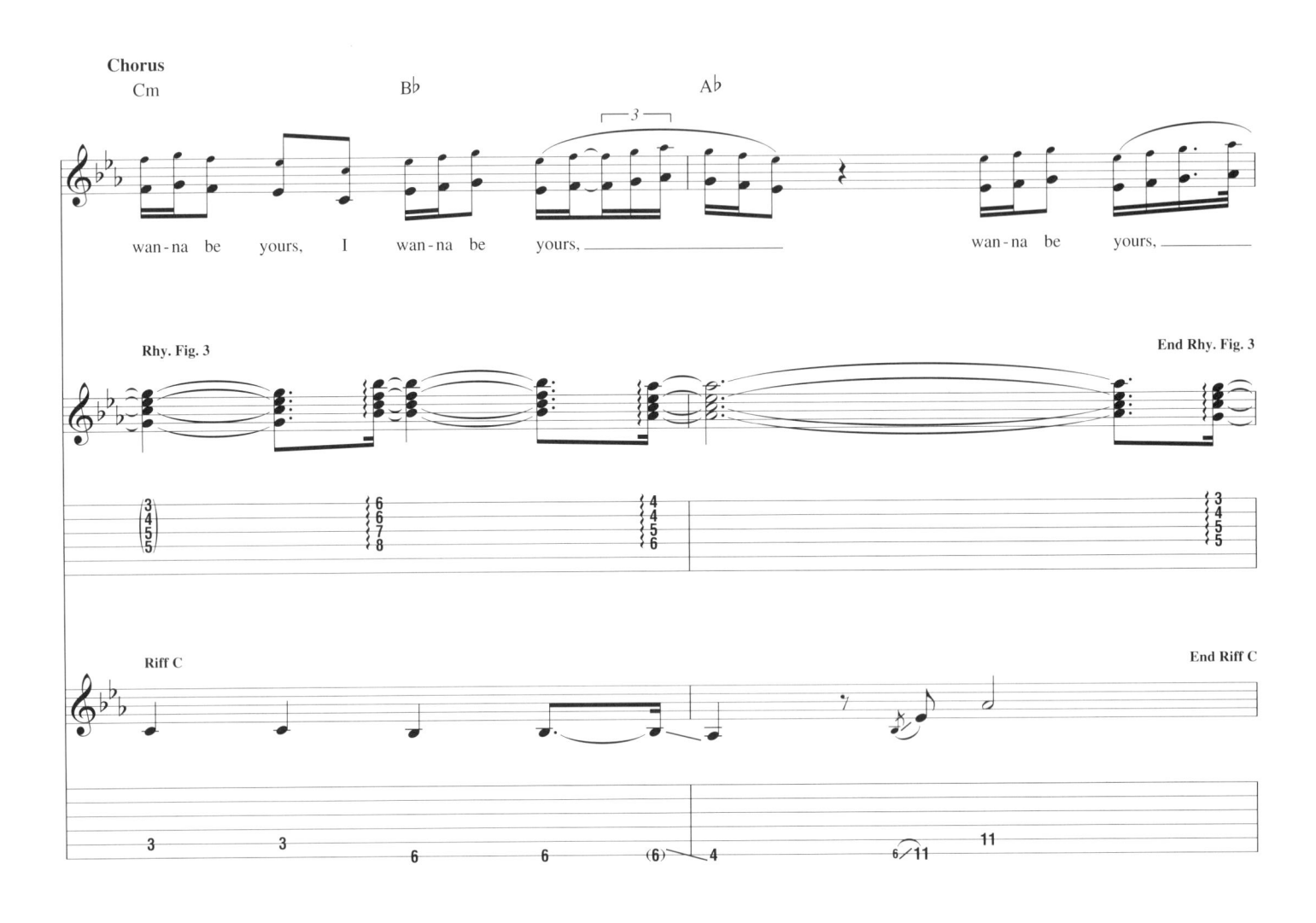

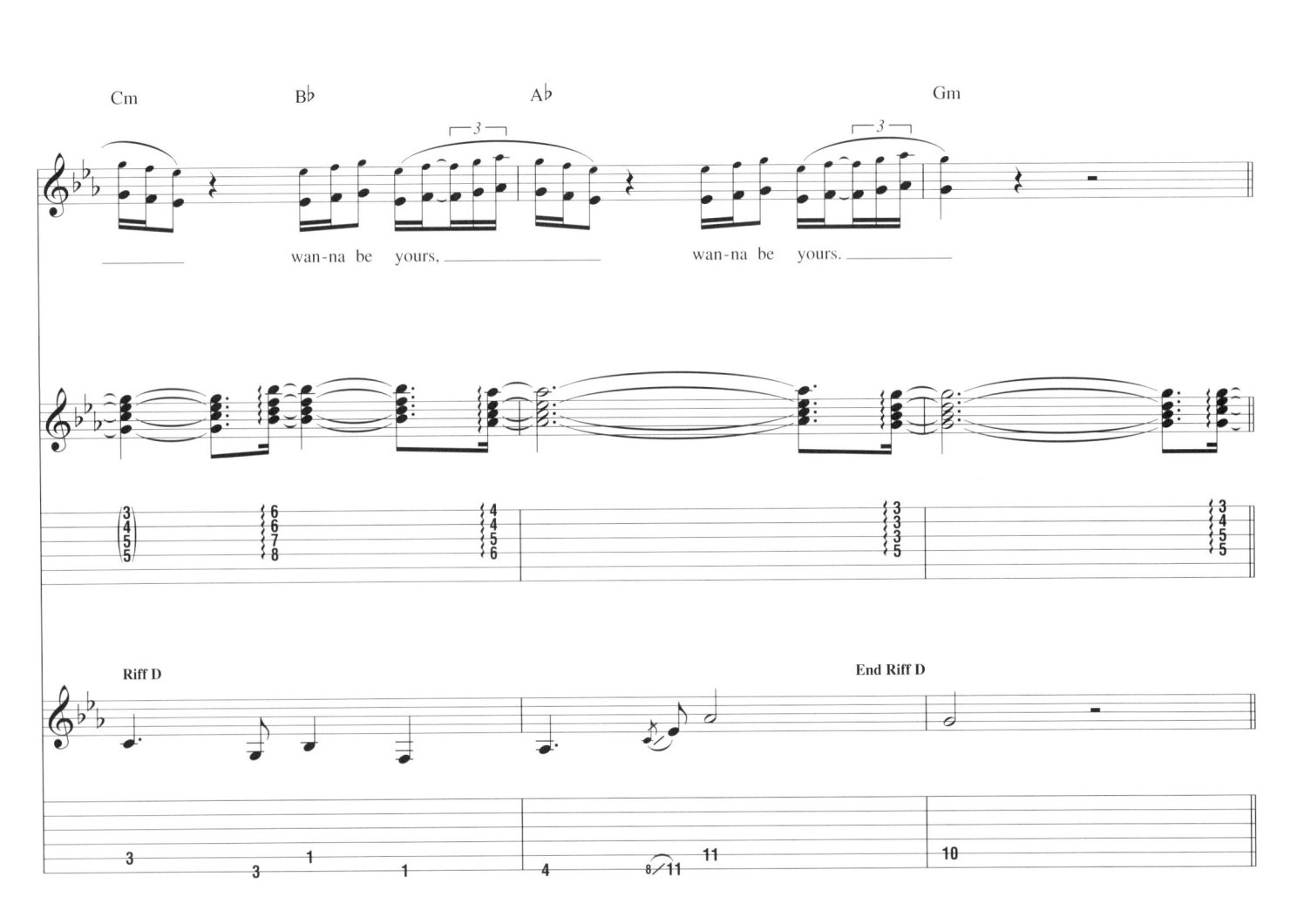

Verse
Gtr. 1: w/ Rhy. Fig. 1
Cm
Fm
Gm
2. Let me be your 'lec - cy me - ter and I'll nev - er run out. _ And let
Gtr. 2
Cm
Fm
Gm
me be the port - a - ble heat - er that you'll _ get cold _ with - out.
Cm
Fm
Gm
I wan - na be your set - ting lo - tion, hold your hair in deep de - vo - tion,
(Wan - na be. How _ deep?)
Gtr. 1
Gtr. 2

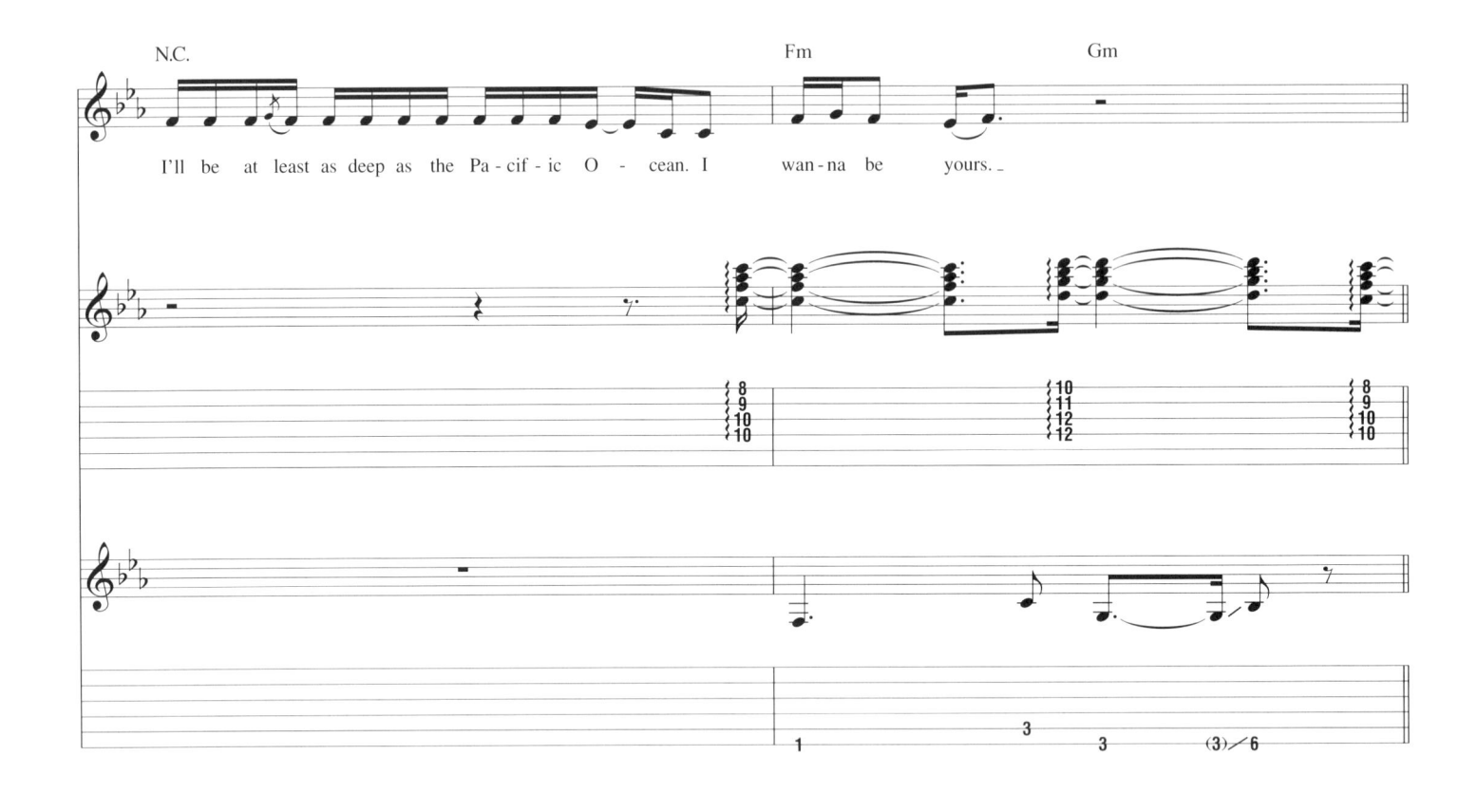

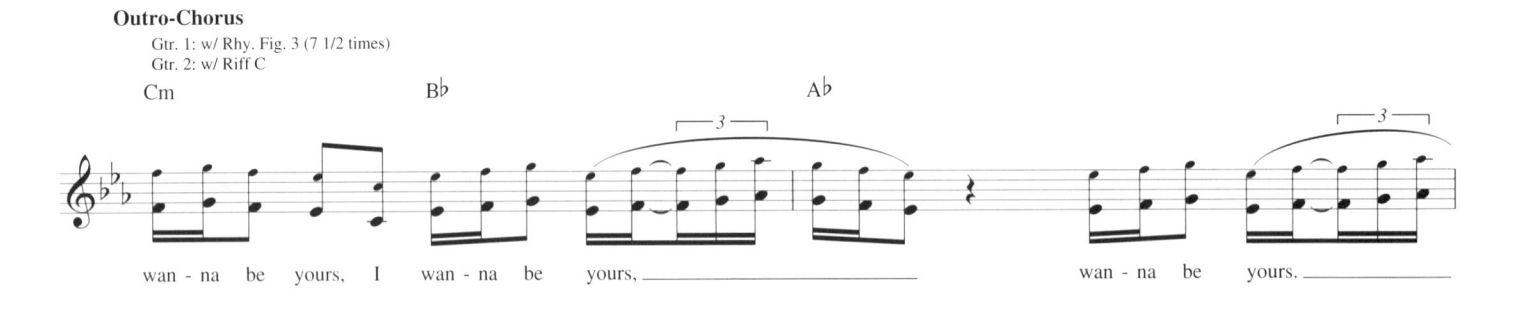

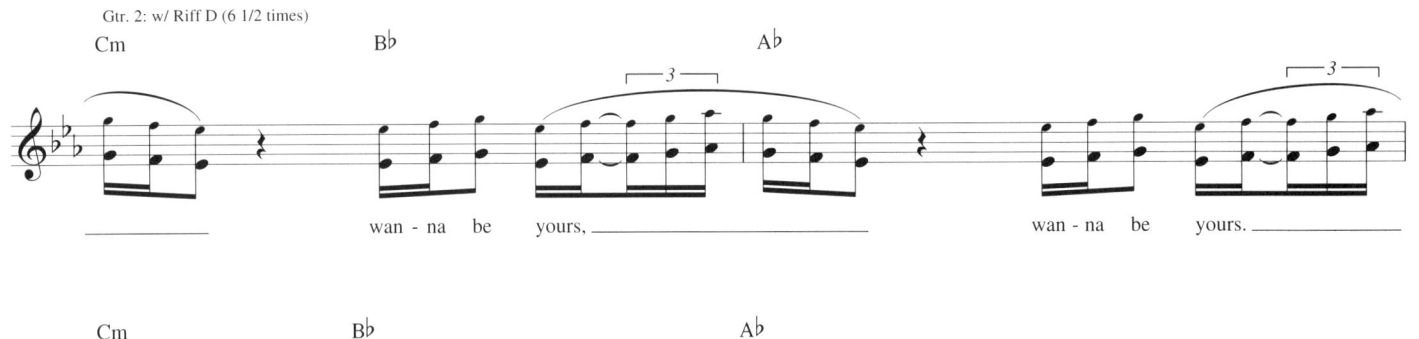

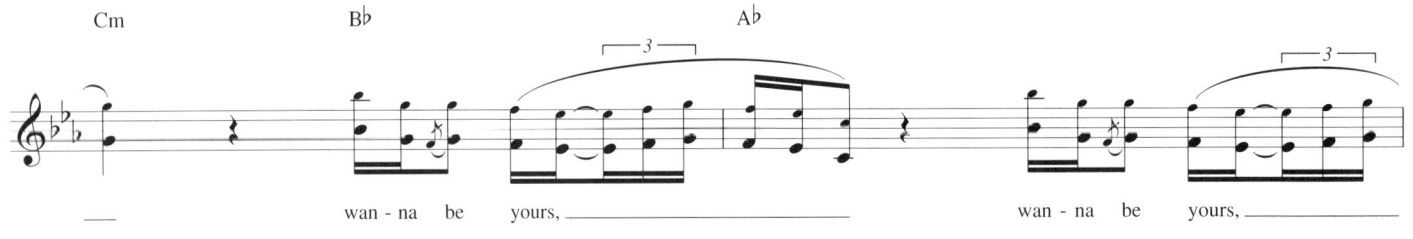

I'll be at least as deep as the Pa-cif-ic O-cean. I wan-na be yours.

Pre-Chorus
Gtr. 1: w/ Rhy. Fig. 2
Gtr. 2: w/ Riff B

Se-crets I have held in my heart are hard-er to hide than I thought. May-be I just wan-na be yours, I

Outro-Chorus
Gtr. 1: w/ Rhy. Fig. 3 (7 1/2 times)
Gtr. 2: w/ Riff C

wan-na be yours, I wan-na be yours, wan-na be yours.

Gtr. 2: w/ Riff D (6 1/2 times)

wan-na be yours, wan-na be yours.

wan-na be yours, wan-na be yours,

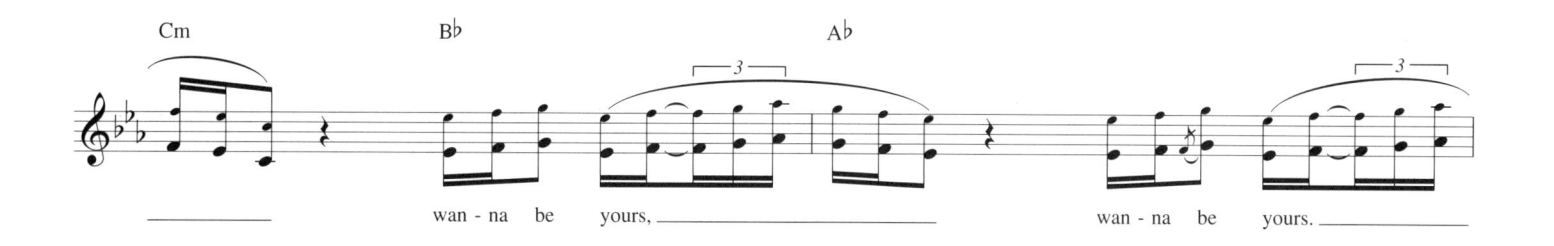

wan - na be yours, wan - na be yours.

I wan-na be your vac-uum clean-er, breath-ing in your dust.

(Wan-na be yours, wan-na be yours, wan-na be yours,

Gtr. 3 (dist.)
mf
w/ heavy reverb

I wan-na be your Ford Cor-ti-na, I won't ev-er rust. I just

wan-na be yours, wan-na be yours,

A♭
Cm
B♭
wan-na be yours, I just wan-na be yours, I just
wan-na be yours, wan-na be yours,
A♭
Gm
wan-na be yours.
wan-na be yours.)
Gtr. 3
Gtr. 1
Gtr. 2

GUITAR NOTATION LEGEND

Guitar music can be notated three different ways: on a *musical staff*, in *tablature*, and in *rhythm slashes*.

RHYTHM SLASHES are written above the staff. Strum chords in the rhythm indicated. Use the chord diagrams found at the top of the first page of the transcription for the appropriate chord voicings. Round noteheads indicate single notes.

THE MUSICAL STAFF shows pitches and rhythms and is divided by bar lines into measures. Pitches are named after the first seven letters of the alphabet.

TABLATURE graphically represents the guitar fingerboard. Each horizontal line represents a string, and each number represents a fret.

HALF-STEP BEND: Strike the note and bend up 1/2 step.

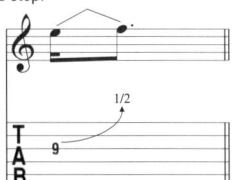

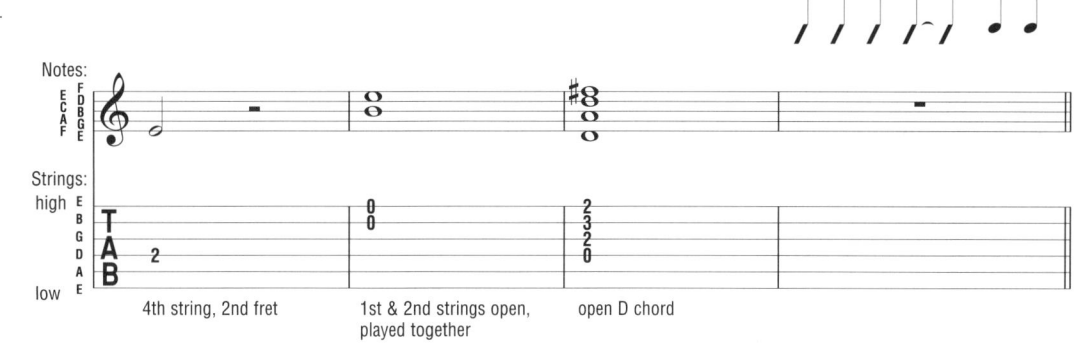

WHOLE-STEP BEND: Strike the note and bend up one step.

GRACE NOTE BEND: Strike the note and immediately bend up as indicated.

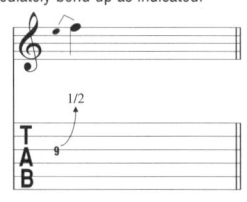

SLIGHT (MICROTONE) BEND: Strike the note and bend up 1/4 step.

BEND AND RELEASE: Strike the note and bend up as indicated, then release back to the original note. Only the first note is struck.

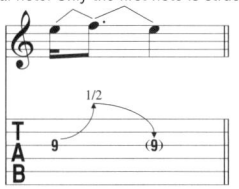

PRE-BEND: Bend the note as indicated, then strike it.

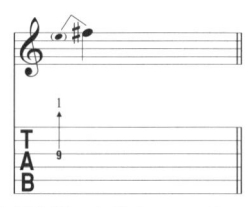

VIBRATO: The string is vibrated by rapidly bending and releasing the note with the fretting hand.

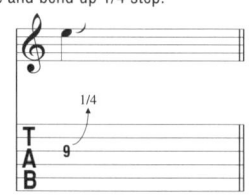

WIDE VIBRATO: The pitch is varied to a greater degree by vibrating with the fretting hand.

HAMMER-ON: Strike the first (lower) note with one finger, then sound the higher note (on the same string) with another finger by fretting it without picking.

PULL-OFF: Place both fingers on the notes to be sounded. Strike the first note and without picking, pull the finger off to sound the second (lower) note.

LEGATO SLIDE: Strike the first note and then slide the same fret-hand finger up or down to the second note. The second note is not struck.

SHIFT SLIDE: Same as legato slide, except the second note is struck.

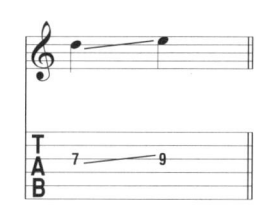

TRILL: Very rapidly alternate between the notes indicated by continuously hammering on and pulling off.

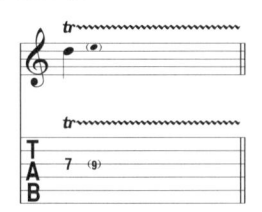

TAPPING: Hammer ("tap") the fret indicated with the pick-hand index or middle finger and pull off to the note fretted by the fret hand.

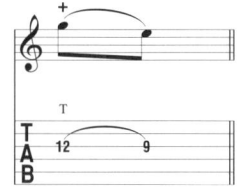

NATURAL HARMONIC: Strike the note while the fret-hand lightly touches the string directly over the fret indicated.

PINCH HARMONIC: The note is fretted normally and a harmonic is produced by adding the edge of the thumb or the tip of the index finger of the pick hand to the normal pick attack.

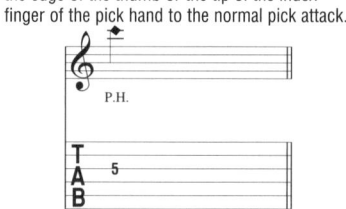

PICK SCRAPE: The edge of the pick is rubbed down (or up) the string, producing a scratchy sound.

MUFFLED STRINGS: A percussive sound is produced by laying the fret hand across the string(s) without depressing, and striking them with the pick hand.

PALM MUTING: The note is partially muted by the pick hand lightly touching the string(s) just before the bridge.

RAKE: Drag the pick across the strings indicated with a single motion.

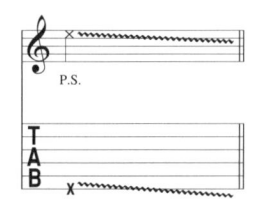

TREMOLO PICKING: The note is picked as rapidly and continuously as possible.

VIBRATO BAR DIVE AND RETURN: The pitch of the note or chord is dropped a specified number of steps (in rhythm), then returned to the original pitch.

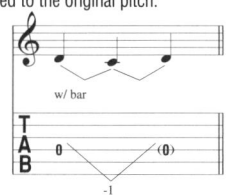

VIBRATO BAR SCOOP: Depress the bar just before striking the note, then quickly release the bar.

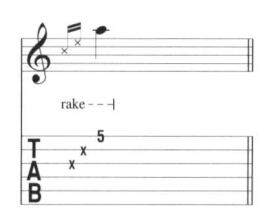

VIBRATO BAR DIP: Strike the note and then immediately drop a specified number of steps, then release back to the original pitch.

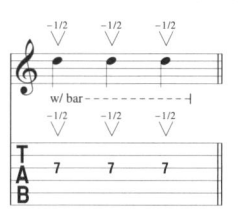

RECORDED VERSIONS®
The Best Note-For-Note Transcriptions Available

AUTHENTIC TRANSCRIPTIONS WITH NOTES AND TABLATURE

Number	Title	Price
14037551	AC/DC – Backtracks	$32.99
00692015	Aerosmith – Greatest Hits	$22.95
00690178	Alice in Chains – Acoustic	$19.95
00694865	Alice in Chains – Dirt	$19.95
00690812	All American Rejects – Move Along	$19.95
00690958	Duane Allman Guitar Anthology	$24.99
00694932	Allman Brothers Band – Volume 1	$24.95
00694933	Allman Brothers Band – Volume 2	$24.95
00694934	Allman Brothers Band – Volume 3	$24.95
00690865	Atreyu – A Deathgrip on Yesterday	$19.95
00690609	Audioslave	$19.95
00690820	Avenged Sevenfold – City of Evil	$24.95
00691065	Avenged Sevenfold – Waking the Fallen	$22.99
00690503	Beach Boys – Very Best of	$19.95
00690489	Beatles – 1	$24.95
00694832	Beatles – For Acoustic Guitar	$22.99
00691014	Beatles Rock Band	$34.99
00694914	Beatles – Rubber Soul	$22.99
00694863	Beatles – Sgt. Pepper's Lonely Hearts Club Band	$22.99
00110193	Beatles – Tomorrow Never Knows	$22.99
00690110	Beatles – White Album (Book 1)	$19.95
00691043	Jeff Beck – Wired	$19.99
00692385	Chuck Berry	$19.95
00690835	Billy Talent	$19.95
00690901	Best of Black Sabbath	$19.95
00690831	blink-182 – Greatest Hits	$19.95
00690913	Boston	$19.95
00690932	Boston – Don't Look Back	$19.99
00690491	David Bowie – Best of	$19.95
00690873	Breaking Benjamin – Phobia	$19.95
00690451	Jeff Buckley – Collection	$24.95
00690957	Bullet for My Valentine – Scream Aim Fire	$22.99
00691159	The Cars – Complete Greatest Hits	$22.99
00691079	Best of Johnny Cash	$22.99
00690590	Eric Clapton – Anthology	$29.95
00690415	Clapton Chronicles – Best of Eric Clapton	$18.95
00690936	Eric Clapton – Complete Clapton	$29.95
00690074	Eric Clapton – The Cream of Clapton	$24.95
00694869	Eric Clapton – Unplugged	$22.95
00690162	The Clash – Best of	$19.95
00101916	Eric Church – Chief	$22.99
00690828	Coheed & Cambria – Good Apollo I'm Burning Star, IV, Vol. 1: From Fear Through the Eyes of Madness	$19.95
00691188	Coldplay – Mylo Xyloto	$22.99
00690593	Coldplay – A Rush of Blood to the Head	$19.95
00690819	Creedence Clearwater Revival – Best of	$22.95
00690648	The Very Best of Jim Croce	$19.95
00690613	Crosby, Stills & Nash – Best of	$22.95
00691171	Cry of Love – Brother	$22.99
00690967	Death Cab for Cutie – Narrow Stairs	$22.99
00690289	Deep Purple – Best of	$19.95
00690784	Def Leppard – Best of	$19.95
00692240	Bo Diddley	$19.99
00690347	The Doors – Anthology	$22.95
00690348	The Doors – Essential Guitar Collection	$16.95
14041903	Bob Dylan for Guitar Tab	$19.99
00691186	Evanescence	$22.99
00691181	Five Finger Death Punch – American Capitalist	$22.99
00690664	Fleetwood Mac – Best of	$19.95
00690870	Flyleaf	$19.95
00690931	Foo Fighters – Echoes, Silence, Patience & Grace	$19.95
00690808	Foo Fighters – In Your Honor	$19.95
00691115	Foo Fighters – Wasting Light	$22.99
00690805	Robben Ford – Best of	$22.99
00694920	Free – Best of	$19.95
00691050	Glee Guitar Collection	$19.99
00690943	The Goo Goo Dolls – Greatest Hits Volume 1: The Singles	$22.95
00113073	Green Day – ¡Uno!	$21.99
00116846	Green Day – ¡Dos!	$21.99
00118259	Green Day – ¡Tré!	$21.99
00701764	Guitar Tab White Pages – Play-Along	$39.99
00694854	Buddy Guy – Damn Right, I've Got the Blues	$19.95
00690840	Ben Harper – Both Sides of the Gun	$19.95
00694798	George Harrison – Anthology	$19.95
00690841	Scott Henderson – Blues Guitar Collection	$19.95
00692930	Jimi Hendrix – Are You Experienced?	$24.95
00692931	Jimi Hendrix – Axis: Bold As Love	$22.95
00692932	Jimi Hendrix – Electric Ladyland	$24.95
00690017	Jimi Hendrix – Live at Woodstock	$24.95
00690602	Jimi Hendrix – Smash Hits	$24.99
00691152	West Coast Seattle Boy: The Jimi Hendrix Anthology	$29.99
00691332	Jimi Hendrix – Winterland (Highlights)	$22.99
00690793	John Lee Hooker Anthology	$24.99
00690692	Billy Idol – Very Best of	$19.95
00690688	Incubus – A Crow Left of the Murder	$19.95
00690790	Iron Maiden Anthology	$24.99
00690684	Jethro Tull – Aqualung	$19.95
00690959	John5 – Requiem	$22.95
00690814	John5 – Songs for Sanity	$19.95
00690751	John5 – Vertigo	$19.95
00690846	Jack Johnson and Friends – Sing-A-Longs and Lullabies for the Film Curious George	$19.95
00690271	Robert Johnson – New Transcriptions	$24.95
00699131	Janis Joplin – Best of	$19.95
00690427	Judas Priest – Best of	$22.99
00120814	Killswitch Engage – Disarm the Descent	$22.99
00694903	Kiss – Best of	$24.95
00690355	Kiss – Destroyer	$16.95
00690834	Lamb of God – Ashes of the Wake	$19.95
00690875	Lamb of God – Sacrament	$19.95
00690823	Ray LaMontagne – Trouble	$19.95
00690679	John Lennon – Guitar Collection	$19.95
00690781	Linkin Park – Hybrid Theory	$22.95
00690743	Los Lonely Boys	$19.95
00690720	Lostprophets – Start Something	$19.95
00114563	The Lumineers	$22.99
00690955	Lynyrd Skynyrd – All-Time Greatest Hits	$19.99
00694954	Lynyrd Skynyrd – New Best of	$19.95
00690754	Marilyn Manson – Lest We Forget	$19.95
00694956	Bob Marley – Legend	$19.95
00694945	Bob Marley – Songs of Freedom	$24.95
00690657	Maroon5 – Songs About Jane	$19.95
00120080	Don McLean – Songbook	$19.95
00694951	Megadeth – Rust in Peace	$22.95
00691185	Megadeth – Th1rt3en	$22.99
00690951	Megadeth – United Abominations	$22.99
00690505	John Mellencamp – Guitar Collection	$19.95
00690646	Pat Metheny – One Quiet Night	$19.95
00690558	Pat Metheny – Trio: 99>00	$19.95
00690040	Steve Miller Band – Young Hearts	$19.95
00102591	Wes Montgomery Guitar Anthology	$24.99
00691070	Mumford & Sons – Sigh No More	$22.99
00694883	Nirvana – Nevermind	$19.95
00690026	Nirvana – Unplugged in New York	$19.95
00690807	The Offspring – Greatest Hits	$19.95
00694847	Ozzy Osbourne – Best of	$22.95
00690399	Ozzy Osbourne – Ozzman Cometh	$22.99
00690933	Best of Brad Paisley	$22.95
00690995	Brad Paisley – Play: The Guitar Album	$24.99
00694855	Pearl Jam – Ten	$22.99
00690439	A Perfect Circle – Mer De Noms	$19.95
00690499	Tom Petty – Definitive Guitar Collection	$19.95
00690428	Pink Floyd – Dark Side of the Moon	$19.95
00690789	Poison – Best of	$19.95
00694975	Queen – Greatest Hits	$24.95
00690670	Queensryche – Very Best of	$19.95
00690878	The Raconteurs – Broken Boy Soldiers	$19.95
00109303	Radiohead Guitar Anthology	$24.99
00694910	Rage Against the Machine	$19.95
00690055	Red Hot Chili Peppers – Blood Sugar Sex Magik	$19.95
00690584	Red Hot Chili Peppers – By the Way	$19.95
00691166	Red Hot Chili Peppers – I'm with You	$22.99
00690852	Red Hot Chili Peppers – Stadium Arcadium	$24.95
00690511	Django Reinhardt – Definitive Collection	$19.95
00690779	Relient K – MMHMM	$19.95
00690631	Rolling Stones – Guitar Anthology	$27.95
00694976	Rolling Stones – Some Girls	$22.95
00690264	The Rolling Stones – Tattoo You	$19.95
00690685	David Lee Roth – Eat 'Em and Smile	$19.95
00690942	David Lee Roth and the Songs of Van Halen	$19.95
00690031	Santana's Greatest Hits	$19.95
00690566	Scorpions – Best of	$22.95
00690604	Bob Seger – Guitar Collection	$19.95
00690803	Kenny Wayne Shepherd Band – Best of	$19.95
00690968	Shinedown – The Sound of Madness	$22.99
00122218	Skillet – Rise	$22.99
00690813	Slayer – Guitar Collection	$19.95
00120004	Steely Dan – Best of	$24.95
00694921	Steppenwolf – Best of	$22.95
00690655	Mike Stern – Best of	$19.95
00690877	Stone Sour – Come What(ever) May	$19.95
00690520	Styx Guitar Collection	$19.95
00120081	Sublime	$19.95
00120122	Sublime – 40oz. to Freedom	$19.95
00690929	Sum 41 – Underclass Hero	$19.95
00690767	Switchfoot – The Beautiful Letdown	$19.95
00690993	Taylor Swift – Fearless	$22.99
00115957	Taylor Swift – Red	$21.99
00690531	System of a Down – Toxicity	$19.95
00694824	James Taylor – Best of	$17.99
00690871	Three Days Grace – One-X	$19.95
00690683	Robin Trower – Bridge of Sighs	$19.95
00699191	U2 – Best of: 1980-1990	$19.95
00690732	U2 – Best of: 1990-2000	$19.95
00660137	Steve Vai – Passion & Warfare	$24.95
00110385	Steve Vai – The Story of Light	$22.99
00690116	Stevie Ray Vaughan – Guitar Collection	$24.95
00660058	Stevie Ray Vaughan – Lightnin' Blues 1983-1987	$24.95
00694835	Stevie Ray Vaughan – The Sky Is Crying	$22.95
00690015	Stevie Ray Vaughan – Texas Flood	$19.95
00690772	Velvet Revolver – Contraband	$22.95
00690071	Weezer (The Blue Album)	$19.95
00690966	Weezer – (Red Album)	$19.99
00690447	The Who – Best of	$24.95
00690916	The Best of Dwight Yoakam	$19.95
00691020	Neil Young – After the Gold Rush	$22.99
00691019	Neil Young – Everybody Knows This Is Nowhere	$19.99
00691021	Neil Young – Harvest Moon	$22.99
00690905	Neil Young – Rust Never Sleeps	$19.99
00690623	Frank Zappa – Over-Nite Sensation	$22.99
00690589	ZZ Top Guitar Anthology	$24.99

FOR A COMPLETE LIST OF GUITAR RECORDED VERSIONS TITLES, SEE YOUR LOCAL MUSIC DEALER, OR WRITE TO:

HAL•LEONARD® CORPORATION
7777 W. BLUEMOUND RD. P.O. BOX 13819 MILWAUKEE, WI 53213

Visit Hal Leonard online at
www.halleonard.com

Prices and availability subject to change without notice.
Some products may not be available outside the U.S.A.